Looking at loss: bereavement counselling pack

Linda Machin

Longman

Looking at loss: bereavement counselling pack

Longman Industry and Public Service Management
Westgate House, The High, Harlow, Essex CM20 1YR
Tel. Harlow (0279) 442601

ISBN 0-582 06801-0

First published 1990
Reprinted 1993

Typeset by Rowswell Haigh Publicity.
Printed and bound in Great Britain by Antony Rowe Ltd, Chippenham, Wiltshire

Contents

Group session notes

* For Session 10 use notes from Session 9

LOSS AND CHANGE

Loss

Bereavement, or loss by death, is only one of the many experiences of loss which is faced during the course of life. While it is important to identify the features which are particular to bereavement, it is also necessary to explore the common characteristics, which occur in many circumstances of loss.

Changing and losing

Loss may be seen in two different forms. First there is developmental loss; the loss which occurs as part of the process of growth and change. For everyone the experience of birth implies not only the living entry into the world, but the loss of security, physical and psychological, of leaving the womb. Clearly this is a fundamental experience of loss for the child, but for the parents too the birth of a baby imposes loss of freedom and changes in life style which have to be accommodated by them and other children in the family. This process continues as the growing child has to leave the security of home to go to school; the adolescent is faced with his/her own physical growth and the challenge of entry into the world of employment (or unemployment); the adult makes choices about relationships and life directions which frequently incur a move from the known into the unknown. The approach of old age, too, with retirement and declining physical capacity can bring uncertainty and fear.

In some of these changes we have no choice – physical ageing – but in others we make choices in the hope of improving our situation. However, even when we have some control over the changes in our lives, we do not necessarily see change as wholly good. A move of house or job may contain many personal benefits but it may also incur leaving behind gratifying aspects of life which cannot immediately be reproduced in a new situation.

Losing what we want to keep

The second form of loss is traumatic loss. Such loss is not experienced by everyone and pain is implicit, rather than concealed, as it often is when it is part of a pattern of change. While people may reflect on traumatic loss and see that new strengths have resulted from their experience, at the time we seldom welcome this kind of loss as having any benefit for us. There are four key areas in which we may encounter traumatic loss:

- Loss through broken relationships, eg divorce or emigration.
- Physical or mental loss, eg disease or disability.
- Economic loss, eg unemployment, bad housing or poverty.
- Loss through unfulfilled ambitions, eg career disappointment or childlessness.

Bereavement: Loss by change, or loss by trauma?

If loss comes to us in these two forms – one as part of change and growth and the other as a traumatic experience of deprivation, how do we see the death of a loved person? Do we accept death as part of life's changing pattern or do we see it as an unacceptable disturbance in the order of things? Our answer is likely to vary with the circumstances of death. If it is that of an elderly person we may view it as inevitable; if that of a child or young adult, then its untimely nature may disturb our understanding of life and death. Modern scientific advances have created an expectation that death of all, except the old, is medically avoidable. This expectation conceals the truth that human life is fragile and that living is an exposure of human frailty; death is a hazard of life which may come as a gentle inevitability but it may come as a devastating blow to shatter the comfortable order of our world.

Patterns of response to loss

The wide variety of loss and the circumstances in which it occurs will produce an equally diverse range of coping mechanisms. However, we do not respond to loss in a random fashion, but develop patterns which we have absorbed as an appropriate means of coping with loss. Patterns which are built up as we grow from childhood to maturity.

i) 'I am consumed with pain.'
There are some people who retreat into their loss and have it dominate their attitudes and behaviour. Such people may have grown up with an unreal expectation that they will be spared experiences of pain. They may have been so sheltered from emotional discomfort that when protection is impossible they can only draw one conclusion, 'I carry this burden alone; no-one else knows what it is like and I shall never recover from it'. Typical of such a response is Queen Victoria, whose life was focused on the pain of widowhood and this pain seemed always to remain with her. Sadly those people who feel separated from others because of the belief that their experience is unique, find it very difficult to respond effectively to other people in their loss. It is a 'coping' style which frequently produces chronic grief.

ii) 'I'm feeling no pain.'
A completely opposite reaction is found in people who deny the emotional significance of their loss. From an early age many children, and particularly boys, will have heard the message 'Big boys don't cry'. They will equate maturity and manliness with the suppression of emotions. What begins as a social justification for the containment of feelings, ends with the masking of true emotional experience. In finding it difficult to acknowledge one's own feelings, it then becomes impossible to recognise grief in other people. Like the first group, lack of sensitivity to others is the result of a misunderstanding about one's own emotions. This response produces a prolonged absence of grief but with the possibility that subsequent losses may trigger a reaction, sometimes many years after the event.

LOSS AND CHANGE

iii) 'I can bear the pain.'
Where people are aware of the reality of their own feelings and have been given opportunities of safety in which to express them, the ability to recover from grief is considerably enhanced. Grief is not all-consuming or denied, but recognised and faced. Such people are then equipped with sensitivity to the grief experienced by others.
While this is only a very broad framework used to illustrate the variety of reactions to loss, it does reveal the way in which patterns of response develop and are expressed. It also explains some of the reasons which produce a particular bereavement response. Clearly, the way we experience loss will shape our response to others.

What is lost in bereavement?

i) A lost physical presence
The most obvious and immediate loss is the physical presence of the loved person. In the past, and in other cultures, much ritual was linked with handling the dead body and disposing of it. Now many people die in hospital and few people see the body of their relatives. In the North Staffs Survey (*see* Session 6), 73.2 percent did not see their dead relative. The need to be confronted by the reality of a lost physical presence is often evaded in an attempt to make the final ritual as pain free as possible. But this escape from reality can impede the process of grief. In situations of war or death at sea, where the relative has no physical proof of death, the commencement of grief may be postponed for years. It is important therefore, that we recognise the crucial need to confront the bereaved with their loss and enable them to say 'farewell'. The funeral service is an occasion when people can begin the painful process of recognising the loss which is suffered.

ii) A lost relationship
While it is important to recognise the physical element of loss, it is perhaps the psychological aspects of a lost relationship which assume central significance in bereavement. The ending of a relationship by death will incur a lost role as a spouse, a parent, a child, a friend. The pain of accommodating this loss is increased because all other on-going relationships will also have to be readjusted. For example, a widow will relate to her children in a very different manner from the way she did before her husband died – she will perhaps be looking to them for practical help or emotional support, which previously was provided by her husband. For the children too, they will have to come to terms with the loss of a father and relate to their mother's changed needs. All this group of grieving people have to rediscover security, affection and companionship which have ended with the death of a loved person. People develop skills or defences which facilitate or impede the healing processes at work during bereavement, particularly in respect of the reformation of relationships.

iii) Loss and spirituality
An experience of loss clearly contains aspects of physical and psychological deprivation, but these in turn induce a heightened spiritual awareness. This is likely to occur even for those who have rejected formal religion or are unclear about their beliefs. Questions about the purpose of life and the nature of death are almost universally posed at the time of bereavement. For some people there may be superficial exploration of spiritual understanding, while for others this might be an obsessive pursuit, which can divert attention away from the other work of adjustment which needs to be made. In some instances a spiritual interpretation will be embraced and regarded as a source of comfort, while in others, to be robbed by death of a significant relationship will be seen in itself as a denial of God.

An understanding of this spiritual dimension is crucial in considering the area of support required by the bereaved. Not that a standard or stereotyped response would be any more acceptable in this area of experience, than it would be in response to the physical and psychological needs of loss.

Summary

Our response to loss will have developed as the result of learned strategies for reacting to change and trauma; strategies which will have been suggested as appropriate by other people, or directly copied from other people or have arisen as spontaneous reactions to new situations. With the variety of loss, which each of us experience through our lives, a pattern of reaction emerges; sometimes this is an appropriate adaptation, at others it fails to help us move forward. Caring for the bereaved requires that we understand the coping strategies, which have become part of each individual's way of handling loss, and use this as the base from which to assist a resolution of the grief caused by the loss.

LOSS AND CHANGE

Divide the line on a time scale which is appropriate to your age. Mark on it times of loss which you see as being significant in your life.

BIRTH ______________________________ PRESENT TIME

Exercise 1.1 Individual profile of loss

GRIEF

Grieving

Grief is an emotion of change and readjustment. It is a response to loss and could more appropriately be described as a struggle rather than a process. A struggle in which the release from pain may be achieved either by evasion or by confrontation. There is a great deal of pressure to pursue the former route as a solution. We value the 'stiff upper lip' and view emotional expression as weakness or lack of control. It is obvious that even for the grief-stricken there are times and situations when it becomes necessary to forego the grieving state temporarily, in order to carry out the practical tasks of living. However, where this practical need becomes a total pressure to suppress emotions and there is no safe opportunity to express feelings of grief, long lasting emotional damage can be caused. Grief is a manifestation of pain and where the pain can be confronted and expressed, the process of healing can begin.

Although grief is an emotion its effect is felt in all dimensions of experience: emotional; physical; social; cultural; intellectual and spiritual.

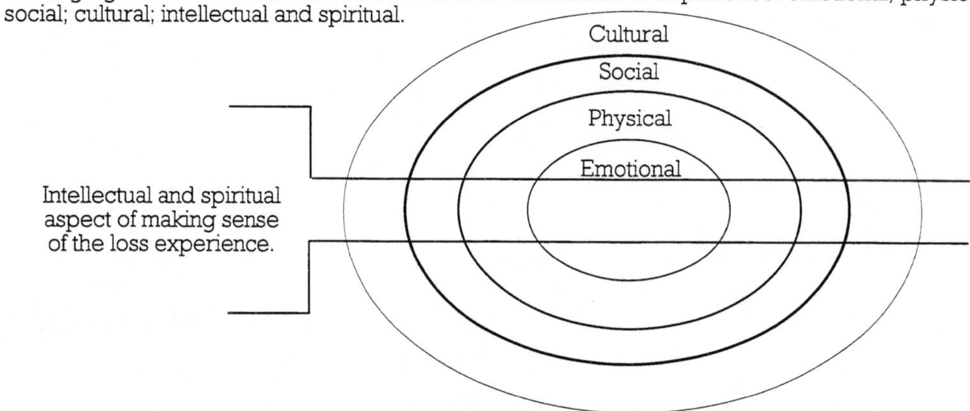

Figure 2.1. looks at the interconnection of these systems, while particular dimensions will be addressed during this and the following two sessions.

Denial

While it is possible to analyse grief and explain it in terms of the psychological mechanisms at work, it is important to recognise the wide variety of reactions which occur within the broad framework. However, the immediate reaction to loss in any form, and bereavement in particular, is denial. There is an inability to absorb the reality of the situation and it is often characterised by a feeling of numbness. This is nature's own form of anaesthetic which protects people from the truth of loss at a time when they are least able to absorb it. Not only does it distance people from the reality of their loss it also can take away the feeling of being in touch with everyday reality.

Pain and anger

Once the numbness begins to subside the pain of loss will become much more real. There is a time of searching in which the bereaved will look for a rational explanation for their loss. This often finds expression in anger. The bereaved feel under attack and express their vulnerability in terms of — 'It's your fault he died.' — thus giving some release to the heaviness of an irreversible loss. The responsible 'third party' may be God, the doctor or the careless driver. In some instances there may be anger against the deceased for having abandoned the mourner to the vulnerability of loss — 'How could you have left me to cope with this alone?' It is clear that in some circumstances blame might be attached to someone, eg the careless driver, but the anger is an equally important emotion even where there is no individual who is literally responsible for the death. Anger is a natural emotional consequence of being powerless and as such should be accepted, not least by the mourner, as a likely part of grief.

Pain and guilt

Anger may be turned inwards in the form of guilt. There may be some guilt about the handling of illness followed by death — 'I should have called the doctor sooner' — or guilt about the nature of the relationship with the deceased — 'I wasn't a good enough husband/wife, son/daughter, father/mother'.

It is easy to recognise the anguish felt when a happy relationship is ended by death, and even in this there is likely to be some guilt, but where an unhappy relationship is ended by death there will be a considerable amount of guilt and regret, however ill-founded those regrets might be.

Facing some of the loss

As the reality of loss begins to be absorbed in the mind of the mourner, there is likely to be a phase of negotiated acceptance. The loss is recognised fof some of the time but is is too difficult to face all the time. When it cannot be faced the bereaved create an element of fantasy in their mind — 'If only we could have had one more holiday together, I could accept his death'. The 'if only' provides an opportunity to muse about life as if the death had not taken place. It revives some feeling of power, in an otherwise powerless situation, by giving the bereaved an awareness of their ability to conceive within their own mind a more tolerable life situation. It is also important to recognise that happy memories from the past can be a source of comfort and strength in the present.

GRIEF

Depression

Perhaps the most easily identifiable element of grief is depression. This feature emerges when the bereaved is beginning to face the reality of loss without a concept of how a new life can be created. Depression is an emotion of despair which comes when reality can no longer be avoided. This emotion is likely to fluctuate over a long period and is liable to be reactivated when a subsequent experience reminds the bereaved about the significance of what has been lost.

Acceptance

Where the opportunity has existed for the bereaved to be supported in facing the pain of their loss, there will be an increased ability to accept the death. Acceptance is not achieved by forgetting the loved person or by premature replacement by other people and activities. It is an integration of the past (and the relationships which made up the past) with the present situation, forged into a new and meaningful life. The new life will not obliterate the significance of what has passed with the death of a loved person, but the bereaved can now bear to lay that aside and focus attention on what has to be created in the present. Happy memories will remain from the past as the pain of grief subsides.

Physical reactions to grief

Physical symptoms are very much a part of the impact of grief. This element may also be heightened as it is often easier to be open about physical discomfort or pain than it is to talk about emotional hurt or distress. It is important nonetheless to see the bodily reactions to grief as part of the overall response to loss and not as a separate factor.

At the beginning the emotional response of denial will be matched by physical numbness and shock. While the emergence of emotional pain will coincide with many bodily symptoms — crying, sleeplessness, symptoms of the deceased's last illness, loss of appetite/overeating, tightness in the throat, nausea — any or several or these will be combined with tiredness or even exhaustion. As the full force of the anguish of grief begins to subside so these physical symptoms are likely to become milder, but with a general sense of apathy and listlessness persisting. With acceptance will come the cessation of physical manifestations of grief.

Grief: Some abnormal features

The features of normal grief, if prolonged, can in themselves manifest some abnormality. While authors will differ as to the time-span of normal grief, it is generally believed that some progress should be in evidence by the end of the first year. That is not to say the grief will be complete: two years is accepted as a likely period for the grief of someone of significance if there have been opportunities for support in the mourning.

John Bowlby has identified three types of disordered mourning in his book *Loss* which looks at the consequences of severed relationships. The first one he calls 'chronic mourning' and it is characterised by despair. It is a despair which is present as an overriding mood of the bereaved and persists after the first anniversary. Such people may be diagnosed as depressed, suicidal or have attempted some mal-adaptive behaviour, eg heavy drinking, which suggests that they are in need of treatment. Characteristic of this group is the attempt to preserve reality as it was before the death of their relative. Queen Victoria is a classic example of chronic mourning. There may also be a degree of self-alienation in which the bereaved fails to recognise help which is being offered to them and can only feel a sense of isolation. Perhaps one should be cautious in making a premature diagnosis of chronic grief as there can be many reasons for normal grief being delayed; it may have certain of the characteristics of chronic grief and yet be amenable to movement and healing not seen when it is truly chronic.

The initial stage of numbness, experienced at the time a death takes place, is a normal form of emotional protection. However, if the emergence from this phase does not involve a movement into a more painful experience of grief then this might be seen as another area of disordered mourning. A 'prolonged absence of conscious grief' is seen by Bowlby as a form of pathological mourning. It seems that this group of people neither seek nor welcome sympathy and support, and pride themselves on being self-sufficient and self-controlled. Unlike the chronic mourner, they will quickly dispose of all reminders of the dead person in an attempt to establish a new and normal routine. For some this normality is achieved by compulsively giving care to other people and locating their own needs in other situations. This condition can go on for a long time, but always leaves the person subject to some vulnerability should their defences be broken down. Another loss or experience of death may activate the previous grief where it has not previously been resolved.

A third situation described by Bowlby is one of euphoria. This unreal sense of elation comes as a result of the refusal to accept that the death has taken place, and is expressed by a strong sense of the dead person's continued presence. Alternatively the loss may be acknowledged, but be viewed as advantageous to the bereaved. For some people the belief that the deceased is with God will incur a denial of the loss and a strong sense of wellbeing which overlooks the emotional and social adjustments which have to be made.

Summary

The process of grief does not take place in a vacuum. Healing will be promoted in people who have adequate social support and who accept grief as a natural emotional consequence of loss. Conversely, people who lack appropriate social support and who suppress their grief, or who have no means of emerging from it, will be impeded in their bereavement recovery.

GRIEF

Psychological process	Physical reaction	Social process	Intellectual and spiritual process
1. Denial/disbelief	Numbness/shock	Almost no capacity to interact socially. Ritual, eg. viewing the body, the funeral etc., play an important part at this stage.	'I can't believe it' Movement between facing reality and mentally reversing reality.
2. Pain and distress – anger and guilt.	Crying, sleeplessness, symptoms of deceased's last illness, loss of appetite/over-eating, tightness in throat and stomach.	Searching – looking and still expecting to see the dead person in familiar situations and in other people. Social contact is a painful reminder of the lost person and of the changed social status of the bereaved.	'Why should this happen to me?' (anger) Recognition of the reality of loss and the anguish of not being able to reverse it.
3. Partial accommodation of the loss – depression, fantasy	Symptoms of 2. May persist in a milder form – apathy, listlessness, sighing.	Some adjustment to changed status, ie, a widow, not a wife. Can begin to consider movement into groups.	'It has happened to me' (depression) A search for meaning.
4. Acceptance	Resolution of bodily symptoms which were related to grief.	Finding purpose and fulfilment in old and new relationships.	Arriving at a meaning which permits a movement from preoccupation with the 'why' of this death to the 'how' of living.

Figure 2.1 Dimensions of loss experience Linda Machin 1986.

SOCIAL ASPECTS OF BEREAVEMENT

Consider these notes in conjunction with the handout showing the overall pattern of grief used in Session 2. (Figure 2.1).

Introduction

Loneliness is often seen as one of the consequences of bereavement. It is a consequence not so much of grief itself, but a symptom of insularity in modern living: small households and social mobility have destroyed stable social networks, which existed in the past and which aided the reintegration of the bereaved. This being so, we must look closely at people's social integration before the death, the level of practical and emotional dependency upon the deceased, their age, social class, the interests and size of family — all of which give information into likely needs in bereavement and the extent to which grief will be a supported or unsupported experience.

Close relationships

Death occurs within a social context. The environment in which the deceased and bereaved have shared their life in the past is of significance to the way in which the bereaved will have to create a new life. Of primary significance to the social consequence of bereavement is the relationship between the deceased and the bereaved. The degree of loss will be far greater where a spouse dies, than where parents die leaving adult children, especially if they live at a distance from the family home. In addition to the proximity of a relationship we also need to consider the quality of the relationship. It is often supposed that the ending of a poor marriage relationship by the death of one of the partners is automatically welcomed by the surviving partner. However, in many cases the surviving partner has difficulty in adjusting to the loss because of the guilt and the realisation that hopes for a more satisfactory relationship have gone forever. Where the relationship has been a good one, in spite of the grief, many strengths exist which help the bereaved to create a new life.

Practical dependency

Practical dependency within a relationship will vary considerably and it is a factor which is of great importance when looking at the potential for rehabilitation in bereavement. The loss is of profound significance where the bereaved is very young, very old, sick or disabled, and the person on whom they depend for physical care is lost.

Women who have been economically dependent on their husbands are likely to have had a marriage based on complementary roles, rather than shared ones. In such a situation, the degree of practical dependency is likely to be high. A new widow may find herself, therefore, unable to do many of the tasks within the home; organising finance; taking decisions, which were previously done by her husband. Conversely, a widower may find household management a very difficult area of responsibility to assume after his wife's death.

Emotional dependency

When looking at the nature of relationships, we must consider the degree of emotional dependency which existed between the deceased and the bereaved; the extent to which the relationship, which has been broken by death, was of primary importance and the extent to which other significant relationships exist alongside it. This will give clues as to the likely outcome in bereavement. Where an exclusive relationship is ended by death, emotional stress arises not only on account of the central loss which has occurred, but because other possibilities for emotional support are very limited.

Role expectations

Some role expectations are based on gender, and clearly response is different for bereaved men and bereaved women. Men are supposed not to be able to cope with the domestic routine of cooking or washing, and offers of help will frequently be made to support him in this. Such offers receive approval and acceptance. However, the widow who may be having difficulty in coping with practical tasks, previously undertaken by her husband, is likely to be viewed with some suspicion if she seeks male support. These are stereotyped social attitudes rather than rational responses to the needs of the bereaved.

Interaction between the sexes also becomes hypersensitive after a bereavement. While conversation, expressions of personal interest and social exchange (such as an embrace when greeting friends) may seem acceptable and go almost unnoticed between married people, such behaviour will cause discomfort and give rise to awkward speculation about its significance when displayed by people newly freed by the death of a partner. Many newly bereaved feel socially alienated because they are seen as a threat to existing relationships.

Age and bereavement

The age of both the deceased and the bereaved require consideration when looking at the needs which are likely to occur after a death. Where death is untimely, ie death of the young or by accident in the old, the denial of the reality of death will produce a heightened grief reaction, which is usually absent when the old or chronically sick die. This is linked to our cultural expectation that we have the ability to save or prolong life until it is socially acceptable for death to occur.

The age of the bereaved will, in part, determine their ability to adapt to a new life. It is often assumed that the easiest death to accept is that of an elderly person. However, for the partner who is alive and who is also likely to be old, the physical ability to pursue a new life could be so restricted that they find it very difficult to come to terms with the loss they have suffered.

Care in the terminal illness

Where the deceased was ill for a long period before death and considerable care was given by the now bereaved relative, the social outcome can be two-fold. First some of the grief may already have occurred in anticipation of the death but secondly social support in bereavement may be limited if care in the terminal stage of illness has resulted in a withdrawal from other

SOCIAL ASPECTS OF BEREAVEMENT

social interaction. The carer, having become socially isolated prior to the death, is likely to feel separated from social support in the early days of bereavement.

Good relationships

For those people who have had the ability to form good relationships, bereavement is likely to produce opportunities for care and support from old friends. New friendships will also come naturally. Those people who have found difficulty in making relationships may find that the distress of bereavement gives additional strain when relating to others around them. Sometimes a marriage relationship where each 'lived for the other' may not so much show that this was an idyllic partnership, but that neither had confidence in looking beyond this one relationship for gratification. A bereaved partner from such a marriage is likely to have problems.

Social integration or isolation

Social integration or social isolation are not merely dependent upon individual preference or ability to form social relationships but are determined by the social organisation in the community. Where the clan or tribe, or neighbourhood are important human groups, the individual will be part of a network that makes use of his/her skills and responds to his/her need. Modern Western society has designed political and economic structures which have replaced these social communities, often leaving the highly mobile, nuclear family unsupported in times of personal stress and distress. While there are obvious exceptions, eg working class areas where families have lived and worked for several generations, or close knit ethnic communities, the degree of social integration will depend on the proximity (geographic and emotional) of family and the extent to which an individual has developed other social contact. Both inclination and opportunity play a part in the pattern of social relationships.

Practical factors in bereavement

One of the major losses in bereavement is the loss of a role and those people who are left with continuing responsibility, eg care of dependent children, elderly or sick relative, are in some ways saved the empty or purposeless feeling felt by many bereaved people. However, being busy can prevent adequate space in which to grieve and come to terms with the loss. Some people may choose to be busy to avoid the pain of facing the gap left by the death of a close relative or friend. Activity and practical demands may suppress the grief, leaving it to emerge much later. This suppression may be reinforced by the incorrect assumption by other people, that the 'busyness' of the bereaved is a sign that they have 'got over' or 'come to terms' with the death.

Cultural/religious support

While the wider Western society may have ceased to offer a supportive, social network, subcultures based on mutual interest or belief still exist, eg churches or trade unions. A strong sense of 'belonging' to a social or religious group will evoke a caring response towards those who find themselves in need of support. The well-being of the individual is usually secured by the group. This will be important amongst ethnic groups as they seek the support of those who have a common religious and cultural background. Familiar mourning traditions will be a source of emotional comfort and social cohesion. For some people this will work well, ie where the size of the group or the bond between its members, permits common traditions and beliefs to be fully expressed. In other circumstances people may want to express their mourning needs through a particular religious tradition but be isolated from a social context in which this is understood and accepted.

Summary

The resources of each bereaved person will depend upon their social background, their present social circumstances and the extent to which there are opportunities to rediscover a new social identity and purpose. Care of the bereaved demands an understanding of these factors and awareness of how to create positive social opportunities for support.

SOCIAL ASPECTS OF BEREAVEMENT

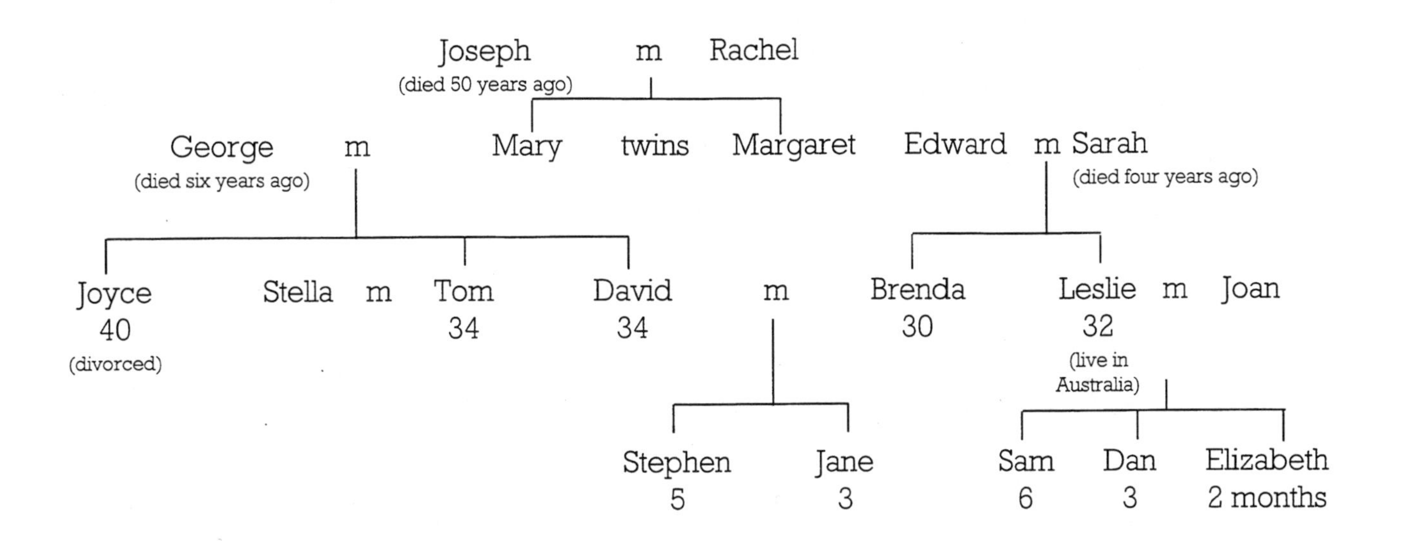

GROUP I - Family information

1. Close knit family.
2. Working class.
3. All live within a mile of each other.
4. David - garage mechanic.
5. Died in a motor-bike accident.

GROUP II - Family information.

1. Family meet mainly for social contact.
2. Middle class.
3. All live within five miles of each other.
4. David - a teacher.
5. Died of a heart attack while playing football.

GROUP III - Family information

1. Little family contact, except at holidays and by telephone.
2. Middle class (younger generation) working class (older generation).
3. Older generation live in town of origin, younger members of the family have moved away.
4. David - junior executive in a finance company.
5. Died of a brain tumour.

Exercise 3.1 Family tree.

MOURNING AND BURIAL CUSTOMS

Every culture develops a philosophy which attempts to make sense of the nature of life and death. However simple the organisation or economy of a group of people, they will develop concepts about death which can be communicated from one generation to another. This belief system or religion, produces cultural practices or ritual to regulate behaviour at times of marriage, birth and death.

Part of the function of religion is to explore the nature of man and to find answers to questions about mortality and immortality. Long before there were written records there is evidence that people believed there was a life after death. The discovery of old burial grounds in which food, tools and manifestations of wealth were placed beside the dead, indicate something of the beliefs which people had about life beyond death. All the major religions have a belief system and a consequent ritual which integrates faith and action at the time of death.

Christianity

A number of variations in Christian ritual exist as a reflection of differing emphases of belief and doctrinal focus amongst the various denominations. Some aspects of the Christian perspective have become part of the wider cultural ritual associated with death even though participants may not give active assent to all the beliefs. Recently however, there has arisen a move to create a ritual suitable for those of no belief or of humanist aspiration. This avoids borrowing from a religious tradition which inappropriately reflects the beliefs of the deceased, but which allows the event of death to be marked with a social act consistent with the emotional need to say 'goodbye'.

Christian emphasis has changed over the centuries as there have been theological moves between focus on the centrality of the hope of resurrection and the grief-laden ritual borne of an uncertainty about mankind's acceptance by God. More recently Christian ritual has combined these aspects - looking at the hope which a belief in a life after death brings, while acknowledging the grief of the mourner separated from someone of importance in their lives.

The funeral will usually take place within a church or chapel and be followed by a short service at the crematorium or act of committal at the graveside. The nature of the funeral service will reflect the style of worship within each denominational tradition, eg Roman Catholics will have a requiem mass while Quakers will have a service with no formal ceremony.

Preference about mourning clothes, flowers and wreaths have become a matter of family choice, although increasingly there is a move away from formal mourning and the purchase of flowers. It is more usual for people to be invited to make a donation to charity as an alternative gesture of sympathy, and messages of condolence are usually expressed by the sending of commercially designed cards.

A social gathering will generally follow the funeral, either at the home of the chief mourner(s) or in a hired hall or pub. The role of the funeral director in arranging for the care of the body before the funeral, the funeral itself, and the social event afterwards, has become increasingly central as individual experience and community tradition in matters of dying have declined.

Hinduism

The care of the dying is undertaken in a religious atmosphere with an attempt to have the last thoughts of the dying person focused on God. This is a continuance of the effort made by Hindus throughout their life to find and communicate with God. The Hindu is cremated and this act is of special significance in that they believe that the body returns to its basic elements of fire, air, ether, earth and water. The eldest son plays a central part in the funeral, usually lighting the funeral pyre while the priest recites sacred texts. Although women would not attend Hindu funerals in India, the tradition in Britain is changing and women will be seen at funerals. Formal mourning lasts for 12 days during which time the family will not go to work.

Judaism

The Jewish faith is based on a belief in one God and their beliefs are contained in the first five books of the Old Testament. Many traditions are associated with death and mourning and remain an important part of Jewish practice. The funeral takes place within three days of the death but not on Sabbath or religious festival day. The body is dressed in a simple white linen garment and is never left alone before the funeral. At the time of burial mourners will put earth on the coffin as a symbol of their involvement in the act of interment. Reform Jews may choose to be cremated but will have their ashes buried in a Jewish cemetery. The immediate family remain in mourning for seven days (Shivah). During this time prayers are said, candles lit, and family and friends visit to offer gifts of food and comfort. Normal life will be resumed after this period of mourning although some social activities will not be pursued for 30 days.

Islam

Islamic belief is based on Allah - the one God and the truth revealed by Muhammed, the prophet sent by God. The worship of Allah is an integral part of Muslim life and so at the time of death the body is turned to face Mecca. The burial takes place shortly after the death, the body having been washed and wrapped in sheets of clean, white cloth. The final prayers are said by a group of mourners prior to the burial of the body. While sympathy is expressed to the family of the deceased the Muslim believes that excessive grief is not the will of God as death is only a temporary separation.

Sikhism

Sikh belief focuses on the oneness of God and the equality of humankind. The body is cremated having been prepared and dressed in white by the family. A prayer is said before the body leaves the home, and after the cremation ten days follow when family and friends gather to

MOURNING AND BURIAL CUSTOMS

continue their prayers and scriptural readings. The death of an elderly person is seen as a cause for rejoicing and will often be followed by a time of feasting.

Buddhism

Buddha is seen not as a god, but as a model for life. For the Buddhist the focus is on the quality of life within and is demonstrated by good behaviour. Their belief in reincarnation is reflected in the funeral and the readings which speak of the release of the qualities of the deceased as a prelude to the the habitation of another being. European Buddhists are cremated and a monk usually leads the funeral service.

These descriptions of religious tradition as they relate to death, give only the briefest outline of what may be the base for the ritualistic manifestation of grief. Rituals may sometimes be expressed within a wider cultural context which gives assent to the religious belief, eg Hinduism in many parts of India, or they may have to be expressed within an alien culture which fails to understand or reinforce what is necessary to a particular religious tradition, eg Sikhism in Britain. In this latter or similar situation, the mourner may abandon orthodox tradition in order to find a compromise which blends past practice with present circumstance. It is important to be alert to the stresses such a compromise may put upon someone who is grieving. Peter Speck sees ritual fulfilling three functions in the process of grief: psychologically it gives a framework in which grief can be expressed; philosophically, it affords a base from which to make sense of the experience; sociologically it provides for shared experience and reintegration of the mourner. These features may be difficult to achieve where tradition has become diluted by a weakening belief system or cultural diversity.

Summary

These mourning and burial customs give clues to the reactions of the bereaved in the immediate aftermath of a death; behaviour is prescribed and accepted in the wider social group. At a later stage of grief when the intensity of emotional pain is subsiding and the mourner undertakes a more active entry into a social world changed by his/her loss, then accommodating that loss will involve an intellectual and spiritual exercise in making sense of what has happened. Belief systems may be reinforced if they are set alongside experience and seen to give acceptable reasons for the nature of life and death. However, some mourners may reject long-held beliefs if, in the face of the testing experience of grief, those beliefs inadequately answer deep questions about mortality and immortality, or fail to afford substaining comfort. This process of making sense is an integral part of grief as reason and faith are explored against the reality of experience; in these circumstances it becomes much more than a philosophical exercise of theoretically making uncertainties certain. Not only may religion be the basis on which sense is made of loss, but folk wisdom and superstition may be used to make good the gaps in thinking and understanding. However the issue of loss is resolved, human beings will always seek to integrate this aspect of their experience by grappling with known and unknown elements which are at the heart of being bereaved; grieving is not a passive encounter with loss but an active struggle to comprehend its part in the broader stage of human experience.

CHRISTIAN ATTITUDES TO DEATH

Old Testament views

Ideas about death are very clearly connected with the concept of suffering. Suffering is not merely a problem because it exists, but because of the apparent injustice involved in the experience; if we all had the same amount of the same kind of suffering to bear, then our understanding about this aspect of human experience would be less perplexing. The dilemma, which seems implicit in any consideration of suffering, is reduced in the Old Testament to a simple equation – sin is the cause of suffering. The challenge to this view of suffering comes in the Book of Job, in which a good man is seen to suffer. The observers of his plight comment and converse with him about the meaning of his suffering. The experience gave Job a new opportunity to reflect on his relationship with God and a rejection of the simplistic formula that suffering is always a result of wrong-doing.

While in the Old Testament there is this very rigid view of the reasons for suffering and for death, there is, nevertheless, a strong source of comfort offered to those who find themselves in situations of distress. The Psalms, particularly, offer an economy of language which goes straight to the centre of human distress. Many of the Psalms whether they are regarded as poems or prayers contain ageless reassurance, which offers much to soothe those who suffer.

Jesus's ministry of healing

The gospel accounts of Jesus's ministry suggest that healing was not only of significance to those who benefited from his powers, but was also a means of communicating his love for people. That love was not about offering shallow, material comfort, but was concerned with attaining wholeness. For some people wholeness came through the recognition that the origin of their suffering was in sin. 'Courage, my son! Your sins are forgiven'. (Matthew 9:2 Good News Bible). While some sickness was still viewed by Jesus as the result of sin, he did not see that as the final punishment, but as a situation that could be remedied by healing. In other instances Jesus seems much more concerned with the state of suffering than with its cause – ' As he saw the crowds, his heart was filled with pity for them because they were worried and helpless, like sheep without a shepherd' (Matthew 9:36). These crowds bringing disease and sickness of every kind were looking to Jesus to give them wholeness.

Jesus raises the dead

In the New Testament there are three examples of Jesus raising people from the dead, and perhaps each illustrates a different response to the needs of the people involved. The raising of the widow's son (Luke 7: 11-15) shows the immediate response of Jesus to the bereaved. She was seen as a woman alone, bereft of husband and child, and Jesus reacted to her need by restoring her son. The second example is the raising of Jairus's daughter (Matthew 9:18-19, 23-25; Mark 5: 22-24,38-42; Luke 8:41-42,49-56). This came as a request for help and brought forth a less immediate response from Jesus. The testing of faith was at the heart of this event. The last incident was the raising of Lazarus (John 11:1-44) in which Jesus delayed his response still longer. He was part of the bereaving group himself as Lazarus was his friend, and so Jesus too was caught in the process of mourning: within the context of his own friends the power of God was manifest.

The grief of Jesus

It seems to be important that the Christian hope of resurrection does not detract from our awareness that Jesus as a man did himself suffer grief. Nor should we believe that for those who mourn, the resurrection hope is an antidote to grief and its pain. People who grieve often feel alone and unsupported. This was exactly Jesus's experience in the Garden of Gethsemane when his friends slept, leaving him to grieve alone. Is there even a hint of anger with the lack of support given by his disciples? 'Weren't you able to stay awake even for one hour?' (Mark 14:37). In common with all people who are faced with pain, there is the desire that it might be otherwise and a longing for events to be reversed. The request of Jesus 'If you will, take this cup of suffering away from me' (Luke 22:42) was that very tension and the desire to be spared pain. At the height of grief there can be anger, both with the pain and with God for allowing such pain to be faced alone. This was also part of the experience of Jesus. On the cross Jesus cried in anguish, 'My God, my God, why did you abandon me?' (Matthew 27:46). For a time, the hope of resurrection could not detract from the pain, the anger, and the dejection, which pervade the feelings of those who grieve.

Resurrection

The revelations made by Jesus did not end with the cross, but were completed in his resurrection and the hope he gave for others to experience eternal life. He had spoken of this in his ministry but his meaning was made plain in the event of his own resurrection, 'For what my Father wants is that all who see the Son and believe in him should have eternal life'. (John 6:40).

Summary

The experience of grief is transformed only when it has been faced and accepted. Assurance for the Christian comes in the knowledge that God identifies with the worst of human pain and suffering and has given complete hope in resurrection.

HUMAN ISSUES

The nature of death

The nature of death has important implications for adjustment in bereavement. Where death occurs after a long illness anticipatory grief and emotional adaption have usually begun to take place. The process of living through the terminal illness of a relative, with the physical decline and accompanying need for medical and nursing care, will have confronted the family with the prospect of death. That is not to say that in some instances the mechanism of denial will operate so effectively as to block out the recognition of (what would seem to outside observers) a very clear indication that death will be the outcome of this illness.

There is a similar process of preparation after a short illness but the initial responses of denial and confusion may not have been sufficiently resolved for relatives and friends to be aware and/or reconciled to the indicators of the terminal nature of the illness.

Where the death is sudden no preparation is possible and the sense of shock will vary with the extent to which the sudden death could be predicted, eg the sudden death of a 90 year old in his/her sleep is likely to be less stunning that the death of a young mother caused by a hit-and-run driver as she stood at the bus stop; being 90 in itself carries some risk of death, being young and standing at a bus stop would seem to carry little risk of death.

One can see, therefore, the shocked reaction lengthens as the preparation for death is reduced.

British hospital care reflects Western culture and it may have problems for anyone who experiences it as an impersonal sub-culture but it may be especially difficult for those who find it conflicts with some of their cultural or religious traditions. Automatic assumptions about willing and easy cooperation in surgical intervention, physical examination, washing and eating may be made without reference to a tradition which would question or prohibit certain practices. The ways in which these variations in practice are acknowledged and respected will contribute to the sense or otherwise of this being 'a good death'. Particular attention needs to be given to this issue in caring for the dying and bereaved in ethnic groups.

Some complicating factors

Alongside sudden death may come the request by medical staff or compliance with the known wishes of the deceased, for the removal of organs for use in transplant surgery. The need for consent by the next of kin at a point when traumatic accident or illness has induced a state of shock or emotional distress will add a further element of stress and anxiety. The time pressure will be enormous and having made the decision two particular complications can arise; first, about the decision itself and the physical mutilation which is involved, and second the sense of the continued life of the deceased through the life of the recipient, a denial of death which is not easily reversed when a mourner has a compelling need to divert from the reality of death.

Anxiety about the mutilation involved in post mortem examinations can also be high especially where for example the need for an autopsy is to establish whether industrial disease contributed to the death; a factor which would determine the eligibility of a widow to financial recompense. Such a widow may find it hard to reconcile financial benefit with the need for her husband's body to be subject to pathological investigation.

An inquest, too, is an ordeal because as a procedure its formality may be intimidating to bereaved relatives; the medical or circumstantial aspects of the death can be distressing, and the time lapse between the death and the inquest may lead to a suspension of the grief until, with this event, the deceased can be finally 'laid to rest'. It is a significant experience of anguish in the journey of grief.

If an inquest can postpone the commencement of grief then circumstances where a death has occurred but no body is found are profoundly disruptive to grief and recovery. The absence of the central evidence of death, a body, allows the bereaved, who has most emotional need to continue in the belief that 'this' person is alive, to behave and often fantasise that this death has not taken place. Similar features of total disbelief may exist when, after a sudden and traumatic death, the bereaved has been protected from seeing the body, and the fact of the death has been removed from the experience of the mourner who cannot, therefore, easily assimilate it into their sense of reality.

Moral dilemmas

These can also emerge when we look at the nature and cause of death. Activities which induce illness such as smoking or injury through sports activity, which may ultimately lead to death, produce a judgement that it could have been prevented. More contentiously, abortion, the rise in drug abuse and AIDS have increased the moral questions still further, because many people see a direct connection between behaviour, which they regard as morally and socially unacceptable, leading to suffering and death. This equation between morally unacceptable behaviour and suffering and death has fuelled the cause of the most dogmatic social commentators and needs very much to be challenged by those who seek to humanise and understand situations of human distress. Here, especially, the pre-existing views and attitudes of the carer must be explored in order to free them from those judgements which obscure the real needs of those confronted by death in these circumstances.

Suicide produced more moral judgement in the past than it does now, but with less harsh pronouncements on the victim comes the questioning and guilt amongst family and friends. Views about the cause and effect are seen to raise issues about who might possibly have provoked such action, or at least failed to prevent it.

HUMAN ISSUES

Scientific knowledge and medical intervention have greatly increased the possibilities for saving life; conditions which previously were fatal can be combated but may, nonetheless leave the sufferer with a chronic disease or disability which is enormously burdensome for themselves and their carers. Questions about the persistence of using life-saving techniques when applied to those whose quality of life is diminished, are to the fore in medical ethics; at what stage should a life-support machine be switched off? Is there a stage when medication to attack infection in the very old or chronically sick should be withheld? One does not have to consider this too long before other questions about actively promoting death to reduce suffering and indignity, are posed. For many the problems of euthanasia lie not so much in the theory as in the practice; who will make such decisions and who will carry them out? Legally what are the civil and criminal boundaries? In all these situations bereavement has an added painful dimension which may come from the griever's own guilt - internalised social judgement - or from the judgement and attitude of outsiders making comments upon the circumstances of death.

Tragic deaths

These bring a particularly overt expression of anger, countenanced if not fuelled by public opinion and perhaps media attention. The finger of blame combined with calls for appropriate retribution are the likely community response to murder, or negligent or criminal accidental deaths. This may seen to give the bereaved an opportunity to express the anger implicit in their grief and yet it is important for counsellors to recognise that a more personal anger, which comes from the powerlessness felt when someone close to us dies, has also to be expressed. The more public anger often becomes self-feeding and results in bitterness rather than contributing to the resolution of grief.

Disasters

Disasters which involve whole communities, eg Aberfan or large numbers of people who happen to be in one place at a particular time eg Hillsborough Football Stadium, call forth somewhat different responses both in the victims and survivors and in the outside observers. For those actively caught up in the disaster, the unexpected nature, the scale, and the destruction and injury, are more overwhelmingly shock-inducing that in other natural or less devastating tragedy. That is not to minimise or disregard the impact of some less publicity noteworthy encounters with tragedy, which individuals and families may have to face. When disaster brings injury, death and other losses, eg home, then mourning for these multiple losses has to take place. For survivors the early euphoria at having escaped may quickly be followed by the guilt at having survived at the expense of, or certainly in the face of, death of other people. This is a feature which can persist for a long time after the event and is seen even now in survivors of the Holocaust. Readjustment to many changed factors can be additionally difficult when the imprint of the disaster itself is likely to remain deeply etched in the mind of survivors and rescuers. The so-called 'traumatic stress syndrome' is a condition which describes the collective symptomology which arises in the face of a disaster. It may be suffered equally by carers and rescuers, who are caught in the exhausting task of responding to horrific destruction, injury and distress. Care for the carers is especially important in these circumstances as the sights and experiences can become psychologically disabling and damaging if not adequately debriefed. The study of the aftermath of disaster has been provoked by the number of such events which have happened in a comparatively short period of time - Herald of Free Enterprise, Kings Cross, Clapham Junction, Piper Alpha, Lockerbie - all of which have brought about a public focus on death and bereavement and in so doing have raised questions about needs and appropriate responses. Many of these questions are practical but perhaps the most alarming ones come at a philosophical and spiritual level as death confronts us with our human vulnerability, which at other times we can ignore in our materialistic and scientific mastery of life.

The location of death

This plays an important part in peoples' acceptance of it too. Where the deceased has died in the place of their choice, the bereaved is likely to feel a sense of satisfaction and completeness about the event, whether it was at home or in hospital. Where the wishes of the dying person could not be met the bereaved is likely to have to spend time resolving their own discomfort, especially if their actions prevented the 'right' location being possible, eg a widow whose husband wanted to die at home, but whose increasing physical needs precipitated his admission to hospital/hospice.

The location of a sudden death or a tragic accident can in itself cause distress to the bereaved – a public place, in the absence of all personal and human comfort. There can be a phobic reaction to the location of death which may have to be addressed in the counselling, eg the scene of a suicide or an inability to go near water after a drowning accident.

The widow

The widow is the person whose bereaved status is most socially evident. The importance attached to the married state and the role for a woman that is consequent upon that, means that her loss is not merely of personal proportions but one of profound loss in her social position. Vulnerability and isolation are often major features of bereavement for the widow, sometimes real, sometimes perceived; sometimes there is not so much an absence of alternative social support as a psychological estrangement from it, because nothing feels like an adequate emotional and social alternative to the lost partner. Younger women who have their own career may not be so socially disadvantaged as a woman for whom 'home' is a career, but nevertheless they will often feel the impact of the couple-based culture on their social acceptability.

HUMAN ISSUES

The widower

In contrast the widower will find his social status little changed by bereavement if he is still a working man; a major part of his life will remain intact and the expectation that he will take initiatives in pursuing a social life and making relationships, potentially reduces his being at the mercy of 'what turns up'. Clearly, there are many men for whom this general statement is not true and they may be even more disadvantaged than a widow, when the nature of their bereavement is not recognised or anticipated by other people.

A widower may be at a disadvantage in two ways:

a) The cultural expectation that he is strong and that he will have little need to express his emotions. The result may be either a prolonged absence of grief, where the defence mechanisms have very effectively suppressed the grief, or a painful struggle to work at the grief while overtly appearing free of it.

b) A wife is often an important agent of communications within the family and her death may not only bring a personal sense of loss to her husband but also an isolation from those other family members - perhaps children and grandchildren whose activities and concerns no longer incorporate him.

Infant/dependent children whose parents die

These children are especially vulnerable. Their physical need for care combined with emotional dependency produces a vulnerability at the point of loss and potential insecurity during their growing up. Bereavement is not simply an event of loss which has to be adjusted to 'now', but a condition producing potential instability throughout childhood and adolescence; a factor which may increase difficulties in the face of subsequent loss or change.

Our grief-denying culture is very inclined to disregard the grief of children; rationalised on the basis of protecting them from the pain of addressing it, or as a denial of the significance of grief in childhood. It clearly is illogical to believe that a person is immune from the impact of loss when it so heightens their vulnerability as a dependent human being. Research (Brown, G. (1982) *Early Loss and Depression: The Place of Attachment in Human Behaviour*, New York: Basic Books) has pointed to the fact that an unresolved bereavement in childhood produces a susceptibility to mental ill health in adult life, thus showing the possible long term hazards of loss in infancy.

The needs of the child echo many of the needs of the adult bereaved person and can be addressed as effectively through listening. The child has the same need to go through the 'story' of the death, especially if for them the story has not been told completely and half truth and mystery surround the events of death. They need also to incorporate memories of the past into the present and the use of photographs, birthday and Christmas cards and drawings afford both a therapeutic opportunity to recall past events and provides a concrete memory link with the person who has died. These could be linked together in the making of a scrap book. Far from 'upsetting' the child, in the negative sense that is usually implied in that phrase, the emotional exercise of moving on in their grief is very healing. It cannot be emphasised too strongly that showing emotion through tears is not a process of disintegrating, but a natural stage of ventilating and externalising feelings, and of appraising the impact of 'this' death on 'my' life.

Fear is likely to be a real part of a child's experience of grief – fears associated with the physical reality of death, fears about the likelihood of other people dying (especially a surviving parent), fear about their own death, and hence their own state of health.

The ability of the counsellor to work with childhood grief will be linked to the perceptions which the adults in that child's life have of the grief, If parents and/or teachers see clearly the normality of grief and identify difficult aspects for the child, they may seek out the help of a counsellor. Where parents and/or teachers are overwhelmed by their own grief, or fail to recognise the reality of grief in childhood, then the child's needs are likely to be ignored. It might, therefore, be a necessary part of the counsellor's work with an adult family member to help them come to see how grief is affecting the children. See Figure 5.1 Adult perceptions of children's grief.

Communication with a child or young person becomes a key element in the counselling process. The child may be unfamiliar with the exercise of conversing with an adult except perhaps for very brief periods. The experience will almost invariably have been one in which there was an implied lack of equality between the participants, eg parent/child or teacher/child. In order to facilitate a positive opportunity for working with the grief, the counsellor needs to work towards an equality in the dialogue – not borne of a false or patronising relationship with the child but arising from a genuineness in the counsellor which allows the child to be himself/herself. Genuineness is essential in all counselling but is especially important with children who may, more instinctively than adults, be aware of its absence.

Toys and pictures can be an affective prompt in the telling of their 'story'. The more abstract area of feelings, for which there may be a limited vocabulary, can come to light with the concrete stimulus of objects and images. Similarly the child's own drawings (children do not have the adult inhibitions associated with a sense of 'good' or 'bad' art) can demonstrate features of the grief. Story books which explore feelings associated with loss can give an opportunity to reassure a child that his/her feelings are normal; many other people have them too. See further discussion about working with pictures in Session 11.

HUMAN ISSUES

Counselling the adolescent is more difficult in that the self-disclosure implicit in the counselling process runs counter to the new-found autonomy of being private or even secretive about oneself. Respecting that blossoming personhood, and yet being available to listen, is a balancing act and it may be that other adults in the young person's network are better placed to pick the time and place when the adolescent wants to talk.

The end point in counselling a child or young person is always uncertain; growing and grieving is a complicated process lending itself to new grief-producing experiences at times of change and loss. Nevertheless reaching a point where the child is accepting his own symptoms of grief, and aware of how to get help, are important stages in discovering internal and external resourcefulness as he/she moves through the stages of his/her own physical emotional and social development. (This section is important to consider again in Sessions 9 and 10.)

Bereaved adult children

Of all the deaths of close relatives which we encounter, the death of parents when we ourselves have reached adulthood, seems to be the most acceptable; it falls within the natural life sequence and we anticipate that we will outlive our parents. It may be more possible to be accepting of this death at a philosophical level, but the impact of losing a person who has always been part of our lives and who perhaps has contributed a major part to our adult stability, can still be devastating. Grief is not only a period of readjustment to the reality of death but is a time in which the relationship with the deceased is reviewed, appraised and relinquished by the bereaved. Such reflection at the time of death raises a number of complex issues about the parent/child relationship:

- What was the quality of the relationship?
- Was the quality apparently good because there was collusion in perpetuating dependency between parent and child?
- Was it good because there was a mutual accommodation of the changes which come with growing up and becoming one's own person?
- Was it bad because there was no emotional and/or social engagement between parent and child?
- Were there external factors which intruded and made the relationship unsatisfactory eg a need for mother to work in earlier years leaving the child to be 'granny-reared'?
- Was there abuse by the parent of the child or later by the child of the parent?

So much self-knowledge comes from the messages, responses, and behaviour which parents communicate to their children. Later messages, responses and behaviour from the peer group, may challenge the early parental values. From this, ambivalence may spring causing confusion and/or guilt: 'Who am I in this world of mixed responses' or, ' I must be bad to have failed to fit into the mould made for me by my parent(s)'. These issues often need to be disentangled in bereavement counselling especially where the emotional bond has been in conflict with the desired freedom of the adult child, eg ' I loved my mother but right to the end she always treated me as her little girl'. Where the bid for freedom was successfully made, much guilt can follow about failing to be 'the child my mother/father would have liked'.
Allowing the adult to disengage from a parent can involve a lengthy counselling process but it can, in some instances, permit a new and creative discovery of the 'self'.

Bereaved parents (infant death)

To lose a child in infancy is one of the most traumatic of bereavement experiences. It conflicts with the expectation that children outlive their parents and with the notion, linked with medical advance, that children do not need to die. For the parents the loss implies not only a lost child, but the lost years of nurturing and a lost sense of future – important gratification in the family life cycle. For bereaved parents the question 'why' is uppermost. A question not so much begging the answer 'because ...' as a cry of profound pain.

Stillbirths and miscarriages are even less understood than where the child died shortly after birth or in the first few weeks of life. In all these situations the assumption of people around the parents may be that no relationship has been formed with the child and the loss, therefore, is insignificant and easy to accept. That planning a pregnancy and preparing for the birth of a child are times of conscious and unconscious preparation for parenthood, cannot be doubted. This psychological and social preparation will have taken place even when a baby dies or where the pregnancy is not very advanced and therefore, to be adjusted to and grieved for as in other bereavements. In counselling such parents are likely to need to take time to reflect on the investment put into anticipated parenthood and begin by engaging with the reality that, 'I was X's mother/father', before they can let go of what has been lost.

Where an older child dies then the reality of the lost relationship has also to be grieved. This may be combined with additional anguish when a child has died from a distressing disease or disability; the demands of caring will have displaced the grieving that was necessary in adjusting to the loss of a healthy child and the recognition of his/her impending death.

The death of an adolescent child is likely to involve the painful review of the conflict and ambivalence which is often a characteristic of the relationship between teenagers and their parents. Accepting this conflicting relationship and recognising that it is part of the natural process of teenagers establishing their own identity, is an important part of reversing the guilt felt by bereaved parents. To have had a tension-free relationship with teenagers may in one sense feel more comfortable but in another demostrates a false suppression of feelings on both sides.

HUMAN ISSUES

In all these categories of child death it is important to see the mother and father as individuals grieving differently, at a different pace and with very different social expectations being put upon them. The high incidence of marital breakdown following the death of a child testifies to the pressures put upon that relationship, rather than the falsely assumed fact that each is a resource to the other partner. Although clearly in some instances a great deal of strength in facing the grief comes from the mutual caring and support of a husband and wife.

Bereaved parents (adult children)

Similar emotional problems will occur for parents who lose an adult child as for those who lose infant children, in that the untimeliness and out of sequence factor are central. For older parents there may be guilt, 'It should have been me', especially where they see dependent grandchildren become motherless or fatherless. For the dependent old, loss of a child may also mean loss of a carer and have important social implications for their practical welfare. As the population as a whole can expect to live longer, the possibility of the very old losing adult sons and daughters becomes greater. It is important to say here that as in other categories of loss, the fact that bereavement is likely to be a more common experience for the elderly does not reduce its effect and may contribute to a deep grief reaction on account of the multiple losses which have to be faced.

Death of a sibling

A child's reaction to death will be closely linked to the accuracy or ambiguity of the information given to them about the death: to the extent of their involvement with the last illness and death; to the degree of acknowledgement which is given to their grief; to the degree and manner of support which they are given; to the way in which the parents are coping. All these factors will similarly apply when a sibling dies. The fear of their own death may be particularly real as they have been confronted with the truth that being a child is not in itself a guarantee that we do not die. This may be combined with an obsessiveness about their own state of health and guilt about the resentments, which arise when a sick child receives more attention than a healthy one, may surface in bereavement. Attention seeking behaviour may be a way of demanding time which hitherto was only available to a dying brother or sister. This behaviour may be counter productive in that parents' physical and emotional strengths may be so depleted that they turn their backs on 'another' child making demands.

In counselling there is likely to be a focus upon guilt and confused identity. The guilt will relate to the ambivalence in the relationship with the dead sibling; an ambivalence which will have arisen during the strain of a terminal illness; and also from the love/hate relationship which is part of the sibling testing of behavioural and emotional responses in the 'safe' family context. This testing out may be fine where brothers and sisters move on to a balanced adult relationship but may produce much anxiety when cut short by the death of a sibling.

Wider family loss

The foregoing sections have considered close family relationships which naturally produce grief when broken by death. However, other relationships in the extended family may have a similar effect. Where there are close bonds within the wider family group the affectional bond, eg between an aunt and niece may have the quality of a mother/daughter relationship. Bonding may have arisen because the role of caring may have been assumed by another family member eg as in granny-rearing. At other times common work pursued by a family, eg a family business, such as farming will have additional bonds to tie family members. This may intensify the grief reaction and simplistic assumptions about the actual family relationship being a distant one may obscure the significance of the actual relationship ties between the deceased and the bereaved.

Death of a friend

Throughout life we may make significant relationships outside the bounds of the family. Much of our time is spent with people to whom we are not related: school friends; friends in leisure context; work colleagues and neighbours. Some of these relationships may only be passing, superficial contacts, while with others there may be a deep though short-lived relationship, eg university friends. Others again may be long-standing friendships of considerable significance. The ritual accompanying death, in the West, is a family affair. Those people who are 'not family' will often find themselves pushed to the margins of recognised mourning and be displaced by family members who have only had a token involvement in the life of the deceased. This is particularly painful and problematic for the surviving partner of a lesbian or gay relationship.

The lack of opportunity to grieve can cause the mourning friend to suppress their grief or to fail to find support in which to express and resolve their grief. Counselling may be such a context where the needs of a grieving friend can be freely expressed. The relationship bond may be much more accurately expressed in familial terms, eg sisters or mother/daughter, etc rather than in the neutral, less specific term of friendship. It will be the nature of these relationship ties which will have to be explored in working through the grief.

HUMAN ISSUES

ADULT PERCEPTIONS OF CHILDREN'S GRIEF	CHILDREN'S GRIEF REACTION
a) *Recognition* that a child's need to grieve is the same as an adult's An ability to accept the reality of childrens' grief, but sometimes a need for help in coping with it.	 Mirror of family grief 
(b) i. *Conscious denial* of children's grief - 'they get over it quickly' 'children adapt easily' 'children are busy with their own lives' 'children soon forget' 'they seem O.K' ii. *Conscious or unconscious diversion from children's grief* 'I need the children to be O.K my grief is all I can cope with' ' I can't bear to face their grief'.	 Diversion from grief 
(c) i. Adults who *control or suppress their own grief* find it difficult to tolerate – overt expressions of grief in children – abnormal/disruptive behaviour in children and will seek help for them. ii. Adults who are relieved to *have the focus on grief located somewhere other than on themselves* may seek help for their children while denying grief in themselves.	 Symptom of family grief 
(d) i. *Overt acknowledgment of the reality of grief* in adult and child members of the family but ii *Covert search for balance* between family members. Children may feel unable to show the characteristics of grief most obviously demonstrated by their parent (s). For example one family member may be angry and another depressed or showing physical signs of grief. Individual members will not show the full range of symptoms characteristic of their grief.	 Compensatory balance between adults and children 

Figure 5.1 Adult perceptions of children's grief Linda Machin 1989

NOTES FROM THE NORTH STAFFS SURVEY

Background

When considering the experience of bereavement, it is possible to learn a great deal from research and psychological analysis. However, the reality of that experience will always be something which is very individual. The North Staffs Survey (1980) was undertaken as a means of looking not only at the broad perspectives but also at the individual accounts of bereavement. It was a survey undertaken by Linda Machin as a means of discovering, within the context of her work for the Lichfield Diocesan Association for Family Care, something of the social experience of bereavement in the North Staffs area. This was seen as a way both of exploring the reality of grief experience and as a prelude to action to increase community support for the bereaved. This aim was based on the hypothesis that with an increase in cultural confusion about the needs of the bereaved support is inadequate or absent.

Taking place from a church base the geographic unit of enquiry was the parish; six parishes were selected to reflect the contrasting social situation of the North Staffordshire area as a whole. Participants in the survey were people who had been bereaved two and half to three years earlier; a time lapse which it was hoped would allow for some recovery and give an opportunity for objective reflection upon the period of mourning and the elements of support/non-support which had accompanied it. The questionnaire took a chronological look at the nature of social activity pre-dating the final illness and death (a means of gauging possible post-bereavement support), the final illness, death, funeral and adjustments during the first year of bereavement. The coding was to be made compatible with computer analysis using the SPSS program (Statistical Package for the Social Sciences).

It is not the aim in this context to look at the methods and results in detail but rather to highlight several individual examples, which emerged in the survey, and see how these illustrate some of the general principles discussed in earlier sessions.

Reawakened grief

It has already been seen that unresolved grief or deep seated pain resulting from loss can recur when some later experience reawakens the old grief. In the North Staffs Survey several people became much more emotional in recalling a past bereavement than they were in discussing a more recent loss (the subject of the survey). One lady in her mid-eighties was fairly philosophical about the recent death of her sister; she felt some sadness and loneliness because her sister had lived with her, but she viewed the death as natural and as the termination of a long and good life. However, she showed a good deal of emotion in recalling the death of a teenage brother some sixty years previously, in a mining accident. Not only were the details clear in her mind but the feelings of her grief-stricken family also emerged.

In another case, a man in his fifties was interviewed about the death of his mother. He was able to recount the events surrounding her death in an unemotional way. When questioned about previous loss he broke down and talked about the tragic death of his son twenty years previously. His wife expressed tremendous relief that he had made this response because he had shown no grief at the time, nor had he ever talked about their son in the intervening years.

An old man talked of coping well since the death of his wife. He had begun the task of adjusting to life alone and assuming some of the tasks his wife had previously undertaken. Some months after her death his pet dog died. It was this event which triggered grief for his wife, although he was not himself entirely clear that this was what was happening. He said, 'I hoped the neighbours would not think I thought more of my dog than my wife'. He was projecting onto his neighbours a possible judgement he was making on himself about the apparent inappropriateness of the timing of his grief.

Families and grief

It is often assumed that each death will produce one main mourner; mistakenly we think that others may be marginally affected by the death but the nature of their grief will be different. We seldom stop to look at the many relationships which have been broken by death and recognise the grief which exists for a whole group of people — sons, daughters, grandchildren, cousins, friends, colleagues, neighbours. The North Staffs Survey highlighted the grieving group in a number of instances.

In a rural parish an appointment was made with a man whose mother had died. He was the eldest son and had agreed to take part in the survey. When the interviewer arrived he was met by a whole family group, some of whom had travelled quite a distance, to give support and to share in what they saw as a family response to a family experience.

It is, perhaps, more natural for us to think of the multiple effect which arises when a child dies; both parents and brothers and sisters are caught in what is often a tragic event. It is frequently supposed that bereaved parents 'have each other' and therefore do not need external support. For many, this double pressure to manage one's own grief and the grief of a partner is too much and the marriage relationship becomes very vulnerable. One couple were interviewed for the survey whose marriage had broken up since the death of their baby.

In another situation parents were interviewed about the death of their teenage son in a motor-cycle accident. Their method of dealing with group grief was to keep alive the tragedy and to hero worship the dead boy. A child born to one of the dead boy's brothers was given his name and other children in the family encouraged to be like him. Grief had become such an

NOTES FROM THE NORTH STAFFS SURVEY

introspective group activity that it was difficult for any one member to emerge and so they all colluded, in a less than healthy way, to contain their pain.

Widowhood

A large proportion of the interviews in this survey focused on the death of a spouse. In legal terms a marriage ceases with the death of one or other partner; in emotional terms aspects of the marriage continue so long as one of the partners survives. This is clearly true when a widow/widower having had a good marriage wants to take valued memories and experiences into the present changed circumstances. However, the past will also impinge on the present for those whose marriage has been less than satisfactory. There is likely to be guilt and remorse about a relationship which is now beyond repair.

A woman talked, within this survey, of her husband's death releasing her from years of unhappiness and misery. Their poor relationship was observed by relatives and friends, who despised the husband for his treatment of her over the years. It was assumed by all that widowhood must be a totally positive state for her. However, she felt unable to enjoy this new liberation because she was absorbed by many regrets for the past. Her need for grief went unrecognised by others and so she had a particularly lonely journey of readjustment to make.

Remarriage after the death of a spouse is regarded by many people as a signal that the death has been accepted and a new phase of life is being undertaken in a positive and fulfilling way. However, too hasty a movement into a new life can indicate a retreat from the pain of grief and produce a veiled burden to be carried into the new relationship.

One elderly lady who was interviewed about the death of her third husband, had already married a fourth time. Her great fear was loneliness and although she was highly critical of her new husband, she felt the situation to be more desirable than being alone. With the ending of her other marriages (the first through divorce, the second and third by death) she had remarried within a few months. For her, each husband compared unfavourably with the previous one, but clearly this was her way of insuring against the ultimate pain of being alone.

These specific cases highlight some of the aspects of bereavement which seem useful to consider as illustrations of individual experience in loss.

NOTES ON PUBLISHED BIOGRAPHIES AND AUTOBIOGRAPHIES

One way of increasing our understanding about bereavement is to read what has been written by those who have experienced loss. The more recent the experience the more likely it is for authors to employ a direct style of writing — a journal, diary or letters. C.S. Lewis in his book *A Grief Observed,* and Prof E.M. Blaiklock in *Kathleen,* quite soon after their bereavement both record, in a journal, the feelings of losing a wife. In a similar way Paula d'Arcy in her book *Song for Sarah* engages in a correspondence with her dead child. In a direct conversational style she is able to convey anger and despair much more immediately than would have been the case had she used a documentary prose. Christopher Leach in his book *Letter to a Younger Son* corresponds with his surviving child about the death of his elder son. A similar technique is also used by H.S. Vigeveno in his book *Dear David* — a series of letters to his murdered son.

Tomorrow to be Brave by J.M. Feehan reflects on the life and death of his wife and combines with it letters written to her after her death. *The Bereaved Parent* by H. Sarnoff-Schiff, and *Blessings* by Mary Craig, both describe the loss of a child. Their writing is much more reflective, giving an account of the death and the subsequent bereavement several years after the experience, and do not seem to need the more immediate forms of communication used by other authors.

A Way to Die by Victor and Rosemary Zorza, *Jean's Way* by Derek Humphrey and *All the Days of his Dying* by Marlena Frick, all look at the commencement of grief during a terminal illness (in each case death from cancer) and show reaction both before and after death.

In reading these books it is possible to see something of the general principles of grief at work, and to recognise also the immense variety of individual reaction.

A PRACTICAL RESPONSE FOR BEREAVEMENT VISITORS

Timing

One of the early problems in making an approach to the bereaved is one of timing. We are aware of the personal and sometimes private needs of the bereaved and back away from involvement in order that we do not intrude. However, it is important to reassure a bereaved person, from an early stage, that people are thinking about them. Notes, cards and letters can be a valuable first communication and have an added advantage that they can be re-read at a time when a bereaved person is wanting support from them. For many people the involvement of family can become less after the funeral. This can often be the time when the pain of grief is felt most acutely and when the bereaved have fewer people around them to listen. Outside support can be particularly important at this stage.

Birthdays, Christmas and anniversaries produce a heightened awareness of loss. Memories of 'what we were doing this time last year' are painful reminders of all the good things which have been lost. By remembering poignant dates for the bereaved and making contact at that time, we offer a very real emotional support at a stage when it is most needed.

Other life crises will reactivate an old grief or bring a more recent one into sharp focus. As friends or visitors, awareness that a resurgence of grief will accompany another death, redundancy, marriage break-up, children leaving home or illness, will alert us to the needs of bereaved people for a long time after a death has occurred.

Starting to look at needs

It can be easier to feel that a real response is being made to the bereaved if there are practical things to be done. While this is true, there is throughout the mourning period, an overwhelming need to talk and therefore to be listened to. Of all the skills which can be offered at this time, the one of listening is the most important.

NB This will be explored further in Session 8 Some general counselling principles.

A practical response to the bereaved for bereavement visitors

Whether we see contact with the bereaved as an informal visit or as a more formal interview, there are several areas in which we should be sure of how to make the most appropriate approach.

Introducing ourselves
In order for maximum use to be make of our concern and interest when visiting the bereaved, it is very important to be clear from the outset who we are; if we represent an organisation, or just ourselves, and what our motives are in making the visit. Sometimes a visit can be less than fruitful because the person being visited is unclear about the use they can make of the contact.

Making a 'contract'
Maximum use will be made of bereavement visits if both the visitor and the visited are clear about the time which is available, the purpose of the visit and the objective for subsequent visits. This is not a formal making of contracts but is a means of clarifying a common objective, and highlights what can be offered realistically by the visitor, for example, state how long you can stay and how often you think you can visit.

Forming a relationship
If we have limited information about the person we are visiting, then getting them to introduce themselves to us can helpfully initiate a relationship through which we can express our support. 'Tell me about yourself' not only allows basic details to emerge, but leads on to consideration of deeper aspects of a person's situation. Even at an early stage in the contact clues may be given about the extent to which the bereaved is coping with his/her situation.

Developing support
During early contact, it is inevitable that time will be taken explaining facts about the person's loss and the relationship with the deceased. The needs which emerge may be practical ones (as it can be safer to focus on specific problems of this kind) such as the need for information after the death. Support in sorting out practical details is clearly very important: the need for help in these areas is much more readily acknowledged and therefore recognised by other people. The area which may go unnoticed or ignored is that of the feelings associated with the loss.

How the situation feels and what ought to be done with those feelings may not be revealed at an early stage of contact, but it is important to be aware of their significance from the beginning. Dealing with feelings at this level is often uncomfortable as it may remind us of some of the pain in our own lives. We should be clear about those things which are painful or embarrassing for us to listen to as this reminds us of our own need in undertaking bereavement visiting. Some kind of individual or group contact is essential as a means of providing the bereavement visitor with the on-going support they need.

What to look for
Bereavement is a state in which grief centres on the lost physical presence and the lost relationship with the loved person. These are combined with a heightened spiritual sensitivity (Group Session Notes 1). Exploring how people cope in these three areas can help us to be clearer about some of their needs:

A PRACTICAL RESPONSE FOR BEREAVEMENT VISITORS

a) Lost physical presence

1. What effect does the absence of the loved person have in day to day living?
   - i) What are the *practical* consequences?
   - ii) What is the financial situation?
   - iii) What is the housing situation?
   - iv) How is the daily routine affected?
   - v) What are the *emotional* consequences?

2. What was the nature of the death — was it sudden or expected — was there a satisfactory parting?

3. Did the funeral help to confirm that death had occurred and did it permit the bereaved to 'take leave' of the loved person?

4. Are there any physical symptoms linked with the absence of a partner/parent/child, such as:
   - i) Sleepnessness
   - ii) Forgetting their absence — setting the table for two.
   - iii) Seeing the dead person
   - iv) Hearing the dead person
   - v) Other

b) Lost relationship

1. What effect arises from no longer being a husband/wife/parent/friend?
   - i) What are the *practical* consequences?
   - ii) What happens with the time that would have spent with the loved person?
   - iii) Who gives advice/care that was previously given by the loved person?
   - iv) Are there any interests and activities which have become important in bereavement?
   - v) What are the emotional consequences?

2. What are the feelings which accompany no longer being a wife/husband/parent/child?

3. What is happening to the other relationships in the life of the bereaved:
   - i) Are they supportive, difficult, non-existent?

4. How does it feel to make new relationships?

c) *Spiritual awareness*

1. How does the bereaved see life and death while in a state of grief?
   - i) What are the *practical* consequences?
   - ii) Does religious practice (church attendance for example) still play a part in the life of the bereaved?
   - iii) Has religious practice ceased since the death of the loved person?
   - iv) Has religious practice commenced since the death of the loved person?

2. What are the *emotional* consequences?
   - i) What is the view of life taken by the bereaved?
   - ii) What is the view of death taken by the bereaved?
   - iii) Has God (or other spiritual awareness) become more real?
   - iv) Has God (or other spiritual awareness) been rejected?
   - v) Does the bereaved feel spiritually supported?
   - vi) Does the bereaved feel spiritually abandoned?

Exploration of these issues may call for a direct question or the facts may need to be uncovered more gently. However, the *practical* and *emotional* condition of the bereaved must be constantly reviewed if we are to understand the areas in which they need support.

Coping with emotional interviews

a) We need to give permission for emotions to be expressed.
b). Reassurance should be offered that strong emotions — tears, anger, guilt, are a normal part of grief.
c) Help can best be given by creating a context in which feelings might be expressed freely, by sitting closer or holding a hand, for example.
d) We must be in control of the time factor so that we do not leave a grieving person in a state of distress at the point when the visit must end.
e) At the time of leaving a bereaved person who has been very emotional we need to focus on something positive. This may be achieved by helping him/her to see that there are things to look forward to, even if they are of minor significance alongside the distress they are experiencing. In this way we can leave the bereaved (particularly if they live alone) feeling that there are short term and pleasurable goals to be achieved: a visit to a friend; buying something new; a 'hairdo'. A more emotional visit will need more time to bring it to a satisfactory conclusion, otherwise we could seem like just another pressure to 'pull yourself together'.

Ending a visit

In drawing the visit to a close it may be helpful to recap on what has taken place, highlighting the things that have been discussed and the progress which has been made in sharing feelings and thoughts. This can help the bereaved to recognise that they have been heard and something of their situation appreciated. It can help them feel some confidence in having used a relationship productively and also lay the foundation for future visits.

A PRACTICAL RESPONSE FOR BEREAVEMENT VISITORS

Future visits

It can be difficult to know who should initiate future contact. Where the bereaved are unsure of the purpose of the visit or resistant to help, it will be the visitor who will have to guage the need for further visits. Several options exist:
a) to fix another appointment
b) to make a formal appointment later
c) to call in casually later

If the visitor decides that the bereaved should take the initiative for further contact then it is important to be sure that:
1. The bereaved feels strong enough to take the initiative.
2. We are not leaving it to them because we do not know what else to do.
3. This is a real means of letting them exercise a free choice.
4. This is the point at which we need to let the case go.

Reflecting on a visit

Even where a visit is informal it is inevitable that we reflect on the content of the visit afterwards. Such reflections are particularly important if there is to be prolonged contact with the bereaved and can be used for the setting of goals. This is an important exercise in considering the needs of the bereaved and deciding how those needs can be met through our visits. In some situations the goals may be fairly minor such as assisting in making a practical decision. At other times it may be a longer term goal or one which is only slowly achieved, such as introducing a hesitant widow into a new social situation.

Principles to consider in making relationships

Three principles to consider when offering support in any situation but particularly in bereavement are:
a) To see people as individuals.
b) To respect their right to make decisions
c) To treat in confidence the things which we hear.

a) People as individuals
It is important to recognise each person as an individual and to allow them to emerge unpressurised by other people's experiences and expectations. To draw too many parallels with the experience of other widows/widowers/bereaved parents denies the bereaved person the opportunity to be seen as and for themselves. Neither should our own style of coping with situations or cultural expectations stand in the way of our trying to see clearly what is happening to a particular bereaved person.

b) Making decisions
It can be tempting when people are in need to assume that their vulnerability makes it difficult for them to make decisions. This can be particularly true when dealing with the elderly. Further distress will arise if people are deprived of making choices for themselves on issues of personal importance. Unless care is taken it can be another way in which the by-product of loss is more loss, with a consequent reduction in self esteem.

c) Confidentiality
If we offer appropriate listening to the bereaved many personal feelings and much private information will be shared. It is essential even if this occurs during an informal visit that information is treated confidentially. Special reassurance needs to be conveyed to the bereaved person that we can be trusted not to share the things we have heard.

This may be difficult in situations where action has to be taken on behalf of the bereaved and in conjunction with other people. We must still be clear that any information we share is strictly necessary in the interests of the bereaved and that they are aware of what it is we need to share, and with whom we will share it.

Skills used in extending concern

The skills we need in undertaking this kind of care are the skills involved in forming relationships. While this is a natural part of our everyday life it is worth reflecting on some aspects of making effective, helping relationships:

i) Observation
So much can be learned by observing a person and their circumstances and thereby assessing some of their needs such as the widower who is neglecting himself; the bereaved mother who seems strangely angry with her other children; the tired face of the widow who is not sleeping. With care, and without making speculative judgements, it is possible to learn a good deal about a situation from the things that we see.

ii) Listening
This is an important skill for those who visit the bereaved. Grieving people have a great need to talk at length and repeatedly about their relationship with the deceased — their final illness, the dying, the funeral. This form of talking is not about conveying information but about relieving pressure at a mental and emotional level. Listening is not simply refraining from speaking but an active exercise of tuning our senses to the need of the other person. The skill takes practise and concentration. Some people find it easier than others to remember details which have been shared with them but it is worth cultivating the ability. People in need of support will enter more deeply into a relationship of care when they recognise that the listener really has listened and

A PRACTICAL RESPONSE FOR BEREAVEMENT VISITORS

remembered some of the personal detail. A feeling of self-worth is always increased when people show that they have committed themselves to the need within the situation.

iii) Communication
There is almost an instinctive fear that we will say the wrong thing to a bereaved person. This in part arises from the misconception that there is a 'right' thing to say and also assumes that verbal communication is most important in this situation. In reality faultering words said with warmth communicate more than cold eloquence. It is important that we recognise the central importance of non-verbal communication: eye contact; touch; facial expression all say so much to a bereaved person whose sensitivity is heightened by the experience of pain. When a situation is known personally to us it can be helpful that we are also seen to have tears in our eyes. The more conscious we are of the need for appropriate communication the more we will reflect on verbal and non-verbal methods of conveying concern and support.

Summary

All those who visit the bereaved need support for themselves. Whether this is done within a group or with another person matters less than that we take time to understand the mechanisms at work within ourselves. It may be that we find it difficult because there remains a lot of unresolved pain from our own experiences. It may be that if we are currently facing loss or bereavement we cannot respond appropriately to the needs of others. To recognise the reality of our own needs is an important step in understanding the help which is required by those who grieve.

NB It is important to recognise that bereavement visiting is different from bereavement counselling, not that one is more important than the other but that they are appropriate in different contexts. Although this section is primarily concerned with bereavement visiting — a response within a community context to the needs of the bereaved — much of the information contained in these notes is essentially incorporated into the more specific task of counselling.

SOME GENERAL COUNSELLING PRINCIPLES

Introduction

Human support is a necessary condition for healing from grief. Traditionally all societies, with very varied cultural patterns, have incorporated a response to grief, a response which sadly has become obscured in the modern twentieth century Western world by a death-denying veneer of invulnerability. As a result discovering new ways of supporting the bereaved has become a self-conscious and often theoretical analysis of needs and solutions. Such deliberate attempts to address this aspect of human experience have not surprisingly produced a move beyond the healing found within ordinary human encounter, in the form of family, community and interest networks, (considered in the last section), to the specific use of interactional skills in counselling. To visit and support the bereaved as a task of natural responsiveness is vital and should be encouraged as the primary source of sustaining those who grieve, but where natural networks for human comfort break down, or where psychological and/or social mechanisms for adjustment do not operate effectively, counselling can be an important option.

Starting points

Valuing the uniqueness of each person who presents for counselling must be the starting point. Implicit within that valuing should be a non-judgmental acceptance of them and their situation in the present while recognising their potential for growth and change. Movement towards change and growth should always come as a result of freely made choices by the client who has been allowed to reflect on the nature of the choice(s) and probable consequences of it/them. All engagements between client and counsellor must be confidential within the context of the agency, that is the client's material should only be shared to the extent of the counsellor's need for support and supervision.

These principles are basic to all people-based work in which the dilemmas of human experience are shared with a carer. Felix Biestek outlines these in his book *The Case Work Relationship*.

Counselling as a particular form of caring is a method of responsive listening in which clients are enabled to reflect on their situation, express emotions and consider and act appropriately upon choices available to them.

This is likely to maximise their recovery from grief by regaining and increasing potential for living life fully and effectively. The counsellor with knowledge about the grieving process and valuing the uniqueness of his/her client may:

i) Allow the client to abandon the counselling prematurely, where their insight and/or motivation prevents them seeing the value of this process to their situation.
ii) Cease to offer counselling when the client demonstrates an inability to benefit from it.
iii) Counsel well beyond the presenting problems when the client demonstrates an ability to work with the broader implications of their bereavement.

Creating safety

While the awareness, interactive skills and initiative will largely rest in the hands of the counsellor, these tools can only effectively be used when the client feels 'safe' within the counselling context. Areas in which safety has to be established are:

a) Counselling environment.
b) Timing (length of session and its position relative to other life activities).
c) Clarity of contract.
d) Trust in the counsellor.
e) Self view of the client.

a) Counselling environment

The counselling environment needs to be comfortable, warm (grieving people often feel cold) and private. Office furnishings ideally should not convey a clinical or bureaucratic atmosphere where the client might feel the control belongs to the counsellor alone. Chairs placed at an oblique angle can allow for the amount of eye contact which is comfortable for the client.

Privacy may be the most difficult of these environment factors to achieve when counselling takes place in the client's home. It may be necessary to address this directly with the client either because they have failed to see its importance to the counselling process, or because consciously or unconsciously they are defending themselves against the exposure of one-to-one contact within the counselling context.

b) Timing

i. A counselling session of about one hour will usually maximise both the opportunity to 'work' on the client's material and for the counsellor's skill to remain completely effective and available for the client. The client's knowledge of this unit of time, together with reminders of it if the content of the session begins to deepen towards the end of the hour, are important.
ii. The timing of a session in relation to the client's other life activities is also important. It is likely to be inappropriate to see a client who is taking sleeping tablets early in the day when the effects of the medication may still be present. Practical caring demands upon the client may also determine times of day which are free to be used for counselling. Commitments which require clear and unemotional reactions such as a visit to a solicitor, an interview with a child's teacher, or a professional commitment of the client suggest that a counselling session before such an appointment would not be desirable for the client.

c) *Clarity of contract*

We have already noted that much confusion arises about the term 'counselling'. Where we

SOME GENERAL COUNSELLING PRINCIPLES

choose to use it we need to be sure that the client is clear about it as a process. In some instances a more easily understood concept of talking one-to-one or time to share their thoughts and feelings with another person, may be easier than trying to offer a multitude of abstract theories to an already burdened client.
The timing of sessions (see above), the frequency of sessions and the overall length of contact need to be discussed. This may have to be done at several stages during the counselling process as revisions in the overall length of contact may have to be negotiated, in the light of the needs of the client and their use of counselling.
The availability of the counsellor between sessions should also be addressed. For example, in the event of a crisis what acceptable arrangements are there for the client to contact the counsellor/agency?

d) *Trust in the counsellor*
i) Genuineness
ii) Confidentiality
iii) Non-judgemental response
iv) Competence
The genuineness of the counsellor will be conveyed, or not conveyed, almost immediately to the client, by the manner in which the counsellor communicates both care and respect for him/her. Whatever the acquired skills of counselling, genuineness is essentially a way of 'being' and should be looked for as a starting point in all those who aspire to work as counsellors.

Overt reassurances need to be given about confidentiality. It may be important to clarify for the client that counselling is confidential within the agency, not just with their own counsellor, though some sharing will take place with the counsellor's supervisor as a means of the client receiving maximum help.

Trust in the counsellor will deepen as acceptance and a non-judgemental response is made to the client. The competence of the counsellor, demonstrated through their confident use of counselling skills and knowledge of the process of bereavement, will add to the client's trust in the process he/she is entering.

e) *Self-view of the client*
The self-view of the client is already likely to have been damaged or shifted as a consequence of losing someone of significance. If this is combined with an already poor self-image, then the client may find difficulty engaging in a helping process where he/she may falsely see the counsellor as the magician whose skills and talents give him/her great power to change and manipulate circumstances, ie the counterbalance to a poor self-image is often an exaggerated or inflated image of the counsellor. This can make the counselling focus unrealistic and the counsellor will need to correct false expectations born of a faulty self-image early in the counselling process.

Listening

Listening is not simply a state of not speaking while another talks, but is a powerfully active engagement with the client's 'agenda':
- Hearing the content of events, thoughts and feelings.
- Appreciating the impact of these events, thoughts and feelings on 'this' person's life.
- Appraising their methods of handling life events.
- Considering the counselling interventions which will help progress the telling of the 'story', and understanding of its implications for the client.
- Adopting a positive regard which will communicate a commitment to the client and an appreciation of the events being described by him/her. In this way *genuineness* becomes part of what is communicated by *listening*.

Giving time

Time is a commodity in short supply; we never have enough of it and many of our activities are disrupted by the pressure to move on to the 'next thing'. We apologise for taking of each other's time and sense distraction in people as they mentally juggle with over-full schedules.

Time takes on another dimension when we are bereaved.
- We wonder whether we have used time past to the best advantage.
- The enormity of our feelings can seem to take us out of the normal time-punctuated pattern of life.
- Questions of time and eternity exercise our minds as we try to make sense of our loss.
- Time is something we would dearly like from other people in order to talk and reflect and rediscover ourselves in the turmoil of change.

It is this latter aspect which is an important part of giving the bereaved time to find a new 'centredness' in an otherwise disorienting life-crisis.

Empathy

When we sympathise with our neighbour we look across to his world of sadness; when we empathise with our neighbour we cross into his world and see sadness from his point of view.

Empathy arises as we stand alongside another person. We can understand more accurately what is happening as we begin to draw on our own experience as a source of enlightenment. We can use our imagination (the faculty of stretching our thoughts and feelings to the boundaries

SOME GENERAL COUNSELLING PRINCIPLES

of both our own experience, and the boundaries of knowledge about people and circumstance acquired through reading and other human encounter) to help us see how the life experiences of the client have contributed to his/her 'here and now' state.
As we get closer to seeing the world of our client from his/her point of view, external judgements about him/her and his/her thinking, feeling and behaviour, become less and less relevant. Our own responses become more sensitive and appropriate to the other person.

Reflecting back/clarifying

Counselling is an interactive therapy in which the counsellor's response to the client is an important way of:
- Conveying the client's value as a person.
- Conveying recognition of the importance of these life events upon which the client is focusing.
- Enabling the client to review and appraise their own particular life-crisis in such a way as to increase their insight, resolve emotional confusion, and devise intellectual and behavioural strategies for handling the situation.

All three of these interactive aspects of counselling are furthered by the verbal contribution of the counsellor. Words need to be carefully used so as not to contradict the listening mode of the counsellor. Words have to reinforce the listening, by demonstrating the care with which the counsellor has received and understood the communication of the client. The process of *reflecting back* is one which the counsellor paraphrases some particular aspect of what the client has said, or summarises a rather larger aspect of his/her communication in order to convey an understanding of the client's material and check the accuracy of what has been heard. This enables the counsellor to come as close as possible to the client's perception of his/her own situation and also helps the client to clarify his/her situation, either by reducing confusion in thinking and/or feeling, or by hearing a restatement by someone outside the crisis. The counsellor, in re-stating some aspect of the client's 'story' may find a phrase like 'Sounds as if . . .' a useful preface to a process of checking what lies behind the client's words.
For example:

Client: ' My husband was a wonderful man. He was the confident, popular one whom everyone admired. He was talented in so many directions. He quite left me behind'.
Counsellor: ' It sounds as if his death is making you feel pretty insecure about yourself.'

Even if the counsellor fails to identify a feeling or perceived reality with complete accuracy (it may have been as accurate as possible with existing information), the client will use the paraphrase as a further opportunity to make clear what lies at the heart of his/her story.

A great deal of counselling work focuses on the emotional state of the client; grief itself, while impinging on all dimensions of experience, is largely an emotion centred process. This being so, the language of emotions is important. However, the language of emotions and emotional self-awareness is often underdeveloped. Some people may use a broad term such as 'depression' to cover fairly transitory sadness, while others use it to convey an all pervading anguish. So there is a highly individual use of words to describe a particular emotional state; the vocabulary of emotion is very variable and descriptively non-specific. This use of words needs clarification in counselling. While we will have a general understanding or a word like depression, can we be certain that when Mrs A uses it, it means the same as it does for Mr B, and will either of them be conveying a feeling that matches with the counsellor's understanding of the word? In the same way that the doctor needs to be clear whether a headache is a sign of tension or a brain tumour, so the counsellor must be clear about the symptoms of an emotional state described by the client.

One way of achieving that clarification is to profile four elements of the emotional experience being described:
- What physical symptoms are associated with 'this' feeling?
- What other emotions are part of 'this' feeling?
- What thoughts are occurring at the time I experience 'this' feeling?
- What behaviour is occurring when I experience 'this' feeling?

Recognising the interconnection of these four elements - physical, emotional, intellectual, behavioural, can help a client feel less confused about what is happening. It also helps the counsellor see much more clearly what the features are for this client, when he/she is depressed for example. It also helps convey to the client the genuineness of the counsellor in wanting to come to a full understanding of their emotional situation. Developing a profile in this way has a further advantage in that it can suggest a route to handling some of the more disabling emotions.

The first of the four elements to address in attempting to reverse the negative impact of an emotion is the intellectual one. It is the area in which the client is likely to see most potential control, ' I may not seem able to choose what is happening to my body, my feelings, or my behavioural responses, but I can still choose what to think'. The counsellor, therefore needs to help the client work at thoughts which contradict the thinking linked with a depressed state, for example. If the first thought which comes with an early morning depressed state is, 'I can't face the day ahead' a contradictory thought may be, ' I only need to look at the next half hour'. What follows from this can be a decision *to act* in accordance with that thought, rather than be paralysed into inactivity by the negative thoughts associated with depression. 'I can choose to

SOME GENERAL COUNSELLING PRINCIPLES

get up and make a cup of tea rather than stay in bed overwhelmed by my depression'. Any contradictory thought which can lead to action empowers the client and is likely to help lift the emotional and physical lethargy of a particular psychological state. Recognising the reality of a feeling without being trapped by it is very important for a grieving person; it reduces the 'victim' state by preventing being overwhelmed by grief or by denying grief's existence.

Goal setting

Goal setting is part of the process which takes the client from 'How things are for me now' to 'How I would like things to be different'.

Clients will always bring, even if in a very unclear form, a concept of what it might mean to be recovered from grief. For some there may be much clarity but no reality, 'All I want is X back', or 'If only my daughter would ask me to live with her I would be all right'. Part of the very necessary adjustment to life without the deceased is to toy with unrealities as a way of coming to recognise the full implications of what has been lost; a process of trying old formulas in new situations and checking out resources to meet changed circumstances.

Part of the goal-setting process is begun by establishing how things are for the client now in terms of psychological pressures and social demands, and then moving towards a greater sense of equilibrium by establishing or re-establishing psychological strengths and social support. It is important to see in overall terms how the client's life is balancing out. Figure 8.1 identifies the elements which contribute to social and psychological stability or instability and hence the areas to be addressed in counselling.

At the beginning the counsellor will be aiming to help the client be more in touch with existing reality. Even this may have to be paced gently where a person's general disorientation or poor self-esteem obscures some of the positive strengths within their situation. It is important too that the search for strengths is not perceived by the client as a denial of the pain of grief, or a disregard of its inherently debilitating nature. The counselling may begin to uncover insight into strengths and leave the client with tasks of testing out reality between sessions. Affirmation of goal achievement is an important stimulus to further growth, for example: A previously strong capable woman now unable to tackle all the practical tasks confronting her as a widow. The counsellor explores:
a) previous capability
b) current tasks
c) helps select priorities and set goals.

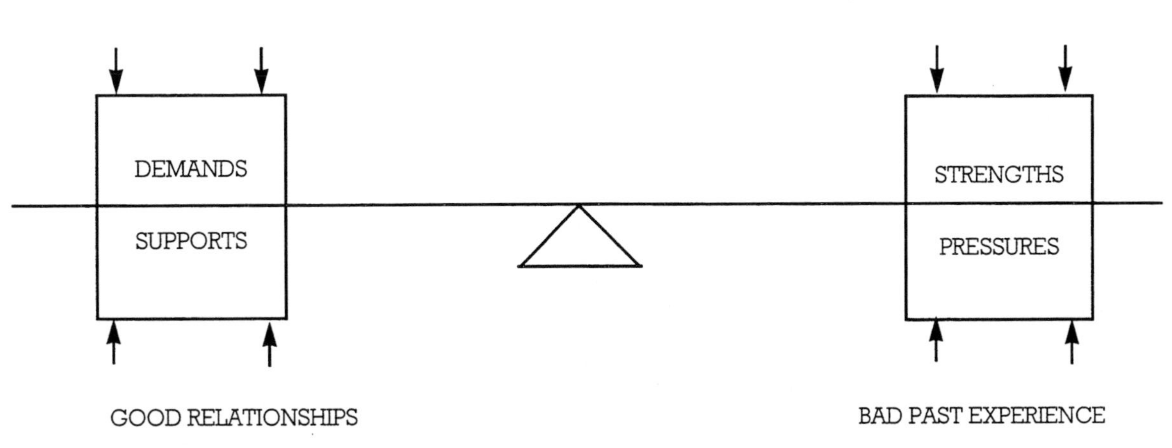

Figure 8.1 Balance of social and psychological stability

SOME GENERAL COUNSELLING PRINCIPLES

The client works on the goals between sessions and achievements are reviewed and built upon in subsequent counselling sessions.

Where internal or external resources do not meet the needs of the bereaved, the focus will not be upon existing reality but will be on exploration of new possibilities for the client. The process of testing out may not be one simply of building up confidence but rather of choosing from a range of possible ways of adjusting to life without the deceased. For example the bereaved adult daughter whose role has been one of caring for elderly parents explores with the counsellor: (a) who she is as a person in her own right (b) what social changes might express her individuality in a fulfilling way.

The answers to (a) and (b) become closely interwoven and it may only be in exploring particular social options that clarity about the 'self' may emerge. The process of uncovering satisfactory solutions may follow thus:

- Options discussed with the counsellor
- Options tested between sessions
- Experience of the options reviewed and appraised within the session.
- Positive options reinforced by building on experience.

Goal setting must always follow the appropriate pace of the counselling for 'this' client. In the early days of grief goals need to be manageable attempts to move against the sense of powerlessness felt by the mourner: small goals promote movement; overwhelming goals paralyse.

Later in the process of grief the counsellor may choose goal setting as a way of challenging a client who seems 'stuck' or reluctant to explore new possibilities. Within an established counselling relationship where the client trusts the counsellor such challenges are an important way of moving away from the familiarity of discomfort, which may seem safer than taking initiatives into untried territory, and into areas which hold long lasting benefits.

Support and supervision

Helping another person face and work through their grief is emotionally demanding for the counsellor. Our own agenda of loss can quickly become tangled with that of our client and we may either use the counselling to give oblique attention to our own needs or else have our feelings stirred and raised painfully to the surface and yet left unattended to. The function of supervision is to explore (a) the client's grief material and (b) the counsellor's techniques; looking at the most effective ways of working with the client and seeing how restimulated material can reduce counselling effectiveness.

Implicit in this supervisory method is support for the counsellor in the task of listening to, and receiving the unburdening of another's emotional pain and/or tragic story. Keeping alive one's sensitivity in this situation demands the clarity and objectivity which is only possible when a third person is available to help the counsellor reflect on the needs of the client and our own needs as counsellor.

It can be tempting to see supervision as wasted time; time when more 'real' work could be done. However, experience shows that the energy liberated by effective supervision more appropriately equips the counsellor both for good quality work and for helping the maximum number of people.

SOME GENERAL COUNSELLING PRINCIPLES

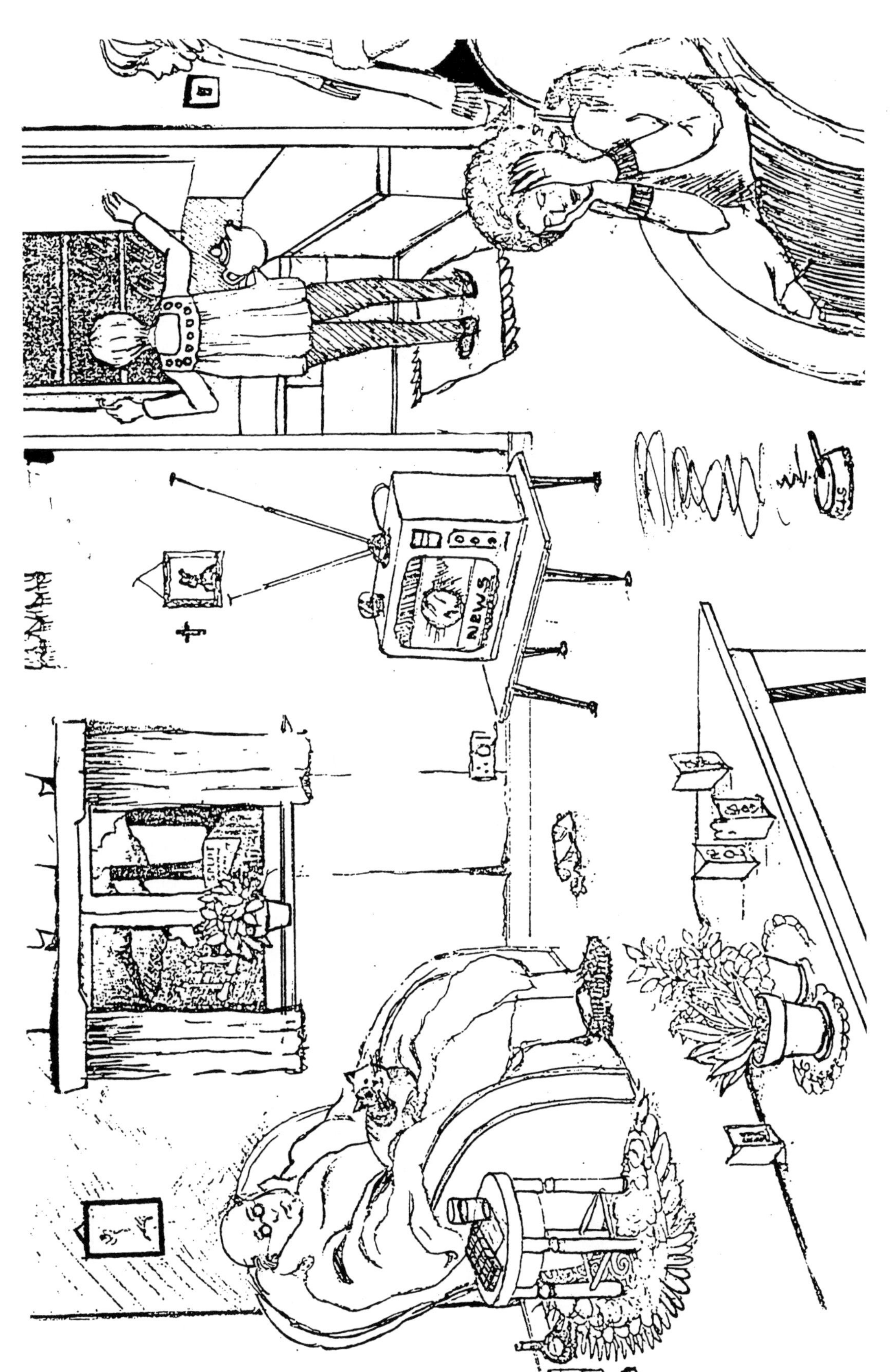

Exercise 8.1 A family setting

SOME GENERAL COUNSELLING PRINCIPLES

In the space provided write down what thoughts and feelings might lie behind each of these statements:

Bereaved mother:
"My husband has a very responsible job. He is always busy, while I'm at home all day with time to think."

Widow:
"My husband took responsibility for all the practical things. He would never let me get involved with financial matters. Now I have to depend on my son-in-law."

Bereaved daughter:
"Dad and I were very close but I don't seem to be able to help my mother. She says that I don't understand."

Bereaved friend:
"We always spent Sunday afternoons together. Either she would come to my house for tea or I would go to hers — that went on for years. We were almost like sisters."

Widower:
"She had been ill for so long but she always pulled through. We've never been apart in all the 38 years of our marriage. We only needed each other."

Discuss the responses and consider, in the full group, how the counsellor might 'reflect' these back to the client.

Exercise 8.2 Reflecting back

GRIEF COUNSELLING

Framework for thinking

Much has been written to increase our understanding about the processes at work when people grieve, that has reversed some of the helplessness we feel in the face of another's grief, by providing us with the information to see grief as a healing process and not one of disintegration. However, William Worden, in his book, '*Grief Counselling and Grief Therapy*' has provided us with ways in which we can actively engage with the process of grief, and be the catalyst for movement through it.

Using Worden's ideas (Figure 9.1 Tasks and goals) identifies the mourning tasks, which have to be completed by everyone, whether or not there is formal intervention by a counsellor or therapist; the goals in counselling which match each of those tasks; the counselling methods which are relevant to the tasks, and the methods which will apply throughout the counselling process. When this counselling process is integrated with an understanding of the broad dynamics of grief in their psychological, social, cultural, intellectual and spiritual dimensions, a powerful body of knowledge becomes available to the bereavement counsellor.

TASK OF THE BEREAVED	GOAL OF COUNSELLING	COUNSELLING METHODS	
To accept the loss	To increase the reality of loss	Help bereaved focus on the reality of the loss by: talking of the last illness; death; funeral	1. Provide time to grieve
To experience the pain of grief	To help the client deal with their feelings	Help identify and express feelings by: exploring guilt; anger;anguish;and allowing them to emerge in rage, tears	2.Interpret normal behaviour/responses 3.Allow for individual differences and styles of coping
To adjust to life without the deceased	To help overcome problems in readjusting	Assist living without the deceased by looking at social and practical implications of bereavement and increasing self-confidence and self-esteem.	4.Offer continuing support.
To withdraw energy from the past and reinvest in other relationships	To encourage the client to withdraw from deceased and look to new relationships	Facilitate emotional withdrawal by: exploring new sources of social and emotional gratification	5.Identify abnormal grief and if necessary refer on

Exercise 9.1 Tasks and goals

Source: '*Grief counselling and grief therapy* by William Worden

GRIEF COUNSELLING

Assessing client need

In Session 8 Some general counselling principles, we considered the creation of an atmosphere, a relationship, and a contractual task, which will be the basis for assisting a client find a healthy resolution to their grief. The establishment of safety, listening, giving time, conveying empathy will all produce in the initial stages of counselling the basis upon which growth may take place. The working basis for the bereavement counsellor comes from a general understanding of grief combined with revealed circumstances, resources, needs and perceptions of the individual client. All these individual factors will need to be disclosed by the client before the counsellor can begin to assess the likely counselling steps to be taken. The questions in the counsellor's mind should be:

1. What stage of grief has the client reached? Bearing in mind that people span more than one stage at any given time.
2. What therefore are the tasks to be undertaken
   a) by client?
   b) by counsellor?
3. What methods should the counsellor use to help the client move forward? Progress here may not simply be a forward move towards acceptance but may involve regression in order to deal with aspects of grief which have been side-stepped hitherto.
4. Do other people need to be involved:
   a) at a practical level, eg where finance or housing are a problem?
   b) at an emotional level, might the client most usefully be helped by involving others, eg family members, in the counselling process?
   c) at a social level eg does the move towards expanded social networks need to involve other agencies?
   d) Does the total picture of need presented by the client indicate that another counsellor/agency should be involved to help eg where the pathology of the grief indicates specialist psychiatric care/treatment?
5. Does the counsellor need particular help in deciding a counselling strategy?
   a) How might supervision generally be used in this case?
   b) How might particular aspects of the client's need, or the counsellor's response to it, require additional supervisory support.

These questions permit a diagnostic approach to the client and begin to indicate a 'treatment plan'.

Addressing grief 'where it is'

The bid for growth and change in clients must never be forced at a pace which is not appropriate for them or which denies them the opportunity to ventilate pain and explore the 'awfulness' of 'now'. This calls for a great deal of sensitivity on the part of the counsellor who needs to judge:

- The depth and extent of current pain.
- The capacity and need to work with the pain.
- The strength of the client to make clear unaided choices about which parts of their grief they want to be addressed.
- The strength of the client in taking next steps.

At this stage one must see the client's perceptions as reality. Ultimately, where there is an obvious mismatch between the client's view and the actual reality of the situation, this discrepancy must be explored. However, at the beginning allowing the client to 'paint their own canvas' gives important information to the counsellor about the insights, resources and context of the client's experience. The kind of discrepancies in perception and reality can arise, for example, when a client sees their problem as one of loneliness. The counsellor needs to hear this as reality at the level of psychological experience, 'I am without meaningful and supportive relationships', but to see that the social reality may be quite different, ' a varied array of contacts and activities'. These contacts and activities may seem insignificant when set beside the enormity of the loss, for example, of a partner. Dealing with the process of making connections with people in one's social world can only begin once the recognition of disconnections, barrenness and isolation are recognised first.

This is one of the many situations in which the adjustments to bereavement at both an emotional and social level have to be made, and in which the counselling has to focus on faulty perceptions.

Next steps

Having established the individual client's starting point, the counsellor can begin to see how the helping process may be used to assist the grief to a satisfactory point of resolution. Using the Worden principles goals can be set (see Session 8) and a 'treatment' plan adopted, providing constant flexibility to the changes in the client's circumstances.

Working through grief

Using focal points suggested by Worden:
1. *Increasing the reality of loss*
This is the focus when at its earliest stage the death is obscured by shock and disbelief. Viewing the dead body and the ritual of the funeral are two ways in which the bereaved already may have been confronted by the fact of 'this' death, although Western practices and rituals in their attempt to protect from psychic pain may not have afforded a complete opportunity to make real the experience of loss. Certainly viewing the body is no longer an integral part of the ritual. Both the personal preference of the bereaved and the proffered opinion of others commonly leads to an avoidance of contact with the body. Without assuming that this is imperative in resolving grief, there are clear signs that where the body has not been seen, especially in the case of sudden death or death in unusual circumstances, the bereaved may be 'stuck' at the stage of

GRIEF COUNSELLING

disbelief for a long time. Where the body is not recovered eg death at sea or war action, grief may remain at this early inconclusive stage.

The counsellor can begin to engage with the natural desire in the mourner to 'tell the story'. As the events of the dying, death and its aftermath are repeated so a process of confirming and assimilating reality takes place. In inviting and encouraging the recall of the circumstances of the death the counsellor is assisting in increasing the reality of the loss. Helping the client use the word 'dead' rather than other euphemisms; accepting the status, eg of widow; preparing for an inquest; choosing words for a gravestone are all dimensions in which reality is confronted. If this is side-stepped in the attempt to protect the vulnerable or masked, perhaps by drug taking, grief will not proceed naturally. Where people have been excluded from the funeral it may be appropriate for the counsellor to help create some alternative ritual which would assist in the process of 'saying goodbye'. With the help of a priest or minister in a church or at a graveside some opportunity can be recovered to allow the mourner to take leave of the deceased. Essentially, the counsellor is working with the natural processes of 'telling the story' and 'saying goodbye'. When these processes have been interrupted or prohibited then counselling should seek to create alternative ways of supporting the mourner in facing these tasks.

2. *Identifying and expressing feelings*
Of all the stages of grief this is the one which runs counter to cultural understanding. For some people the contrived appearance of emotionless 'strength' may work and exclude the grief, but for others it becomes a struggle for mastery over the very natural feelings of anguish. The counsellor will need to spend some time talking about the role of emotions in grief if the client is not to see the counselling as a subversive attack on his/her attempts to be brave and coping.

Helping to identify and express feelings requires a good deal of safety within the counselling relationship especially if this is an isolated opportunity to let go of emotions ordinarily controlled and contained. It is not enough for the counsellor to feel comfortable with the expression of feelings; the client also must recognise and feel the appropriateness of emotional release. There is likely to be a great variation in the ease with which clients express their feelings through tears, even though there may be recognition that it is an important part of ventilating pent up emotion. However, the feeling of anger will usually cause more anxiety in that it is not recognised as the natural emotional response to powerlessness, but rather as a potentially damaging prelude to aggressive or inappropriate behaviour. Clients need help in being able to separate the feeling,which is a neutral and natural consequence of bereavement, from action which can be a chosen response rather than a reflexive reaction. Very often the anger felt by a grieving person is quickly met by the reasoned rationalisation of those around them in an attempt to diffuse any out of control expression of it. This only serves to suppress the anger. Counselling is an appropriate forum where the client can give voice to the anger by finding the words and giving vocal expression to it. Physical activity such as beating a cushion or vigorous exercise can also help to release the energy created by anger. In these ways anger can safely be expressed and thus dissipated.

Guilt is another of grief's emotions which again needs to be expressed and not suppressed by a hasty overlay of reassurance by family and friends who recognise the more objective reality. Guilt about the manner of the death and dying and/or about the nature of the relationship with the deceased are very central themes in bereavement counselling. The range of inadequacy felt by the bereaved should be fully expressed. The counsellor importantly must point out to the client that his/her passive reception of the catalogue of shortcomings is to allow what needs to be expressed to emerge rather than an acceptance of the accuracy of the self-judgements being made. When this has been done the client should be encouraged to explore all those ways in which his/her actions and responses were appropriate, caring and sustaining to the deceased. In this way the bereaved can be encouraged to build up a balance sheet; having readily completed the debit side of the account he/she can be prompted to explore the credit side, and then come to see for themselves the reality. This is a much more powerful contradiction to guilt than an external denial of its appropriateness.

Sometimes there may be justifiable guilt in which a known hurt may have been caused to the deceased. Allowing the client to say sorry as if to the deceased, and also to speculate as to the deceased's response (which will often be much more forgiving than the client will be to himself/herself) is very important. These powerful feelings can seem overwhelming at certain stages in the grief. Exploring them in the counselling context can help diffuse them. For clients whose grief has become chronic, ie there are various reasons for them to stay with the pain of grief, help should be given to assist in letting go and moving away from the pain. For others they may need temporary relief and using a relaxation exercise at the end of the counselling engagement can be useful (see session 11).

3. *Overcoming problems in re-adjusting*
This is a stage at which the client is less focused upon the internal aspects of their grief but is attending to the social consequences of their loss. The practical implications of modifying life-style can be very variable; for some little will change; for others financial hardship, moving house, getting a job may follow from their bereavement. Decision making is difficult and so the counselling can afford an important opportunity to think about options and to look at the range of choices; reflecting on any current experience which helps sort out an appropriate choice.

GRIEF COUNSELLING

At this point the encounter between the mourner and the world will be largely affected by the self-image of the griever. Where the person who died was the only source of personal affirmation then the client will not only have lost a person to death but also the reference point for himself/herself. Relationships which have been very exclusive leave the bereaved with few sustaining emotional connections to give them the confidence to be themselves and discover a new range of social contacts. Counselling can assist the client in this process of establishing self-esteem as the prelude to re-entry into a new phase of living. Asking the client what they like about themselves can give a good idea of the ego strength they have in working at the social consequences of loss. Helping them appraise their strengths, which undoubtedly always exist, is an important part of developing their resourcefulness.

It is often at this stage too that the client is trying to make sense of their loss. In facing some of the wider questions raised by death some people may find reading books useful (only recommend books that you have read and seem appropriate to 'this' client), joining self-help groups and meeting with people in similar circumstances, talking with a priest, all can be ways of aiding the client's natural search for meaning.

4. *Withdrawing from the deceased and entering a new phase of living*
This will be the natural end result of having worked through the others aspects of grief - denial, pain, readjustment. Often the counselling will have ceased before this phase is complete; the client will probably have already glimpsed the new possibilities and so have the strength to move to this point alone or with the support of their natural social networks. However, time may need to be spent with a client who has unrealistic expectations of this end point; either imagining some magical transformation in their situation or conversely believing the barrenness of mourning will always persist. Discovering new forms of gratification from old relationships can be a significant step beyond grief realising that a 'new phase in life' does not always mean setting off into the glow of a Hollywood sunset with new and exciting people! Appreciating this is especially important for older people who even within the limitations of a restricted physical and/or social situation, can find sources of happiness and gratification. For example discovering the warm companionship of a grandchild may not be a substitute for a partner, but can bring a new and different kind of joy.

Where is counselling appropriate?

If the new specialism of bereavement counselling is not to accelerate the view held by many people in Western society, that grief can only be handled by the experts, then it must identify those circumstances where it is appropriate and in other situations reinforce the innate caring resources within the social networks of bereaved people.

Three categories of need seem to suggest counselling intervention:

1. Situations of tragic bereavement where the nature of the death itself produces particular problems in adjustment, eg murder, suicide, group disaster, accidents or untimely deaths. In this, more than in other situations, recognition is given to the psychological trauma which has to be addressed and the pressure to 'get on with life' is not so harshly applied.

2. Situations of social isolation may also require counselling support where people find themselves without the opportunity to use others as a sounding-board for their thoughts and feelings, and as a means of social support and comfort.

This is a category of need often found in the elderly or where people have recently moved to a new area.

3. Counselling may also be appropriate where people are dealing with multiple problems, the bereavement being one. In this situation, the stress of handling more than one crisis is likely to deplete the resources which are available for resolving the grief.

GRIEF COUNSELLING

1. Who was the main communicator?

2. What was it he/she was saying?

3. What was it he/she was feeling?

4. What was the receiver saying?

5 What was he/she feeling?

6. What can we say about their relationship?

7. What help is needed?

Exercise 9.1 Role play debriefing sheet

GRIEF COUNSELLING

1. What is the client saying?

2. What is the client feeling?

3. What approach did you/would you use?

4. Did it work?

5. What could have been done differently?

6. What stage of grief has this client reached?

7. What next steps would you want to take?

8. What long term goals might you set?

9. What help might you want in working with this client?

Exercise 9.2 Role play debriefing sheet

GRIEF COUNSELLING

1. What is the client saying?

2. What is the client feeling?

3. What approach did you/would you use?

4. Did it work?

5. What could have been done differently ?

6. What stage of grief has this client reached?

7. What next steps would you want to take ?

8. What long term goals might you set?

9. What help might you want in working with this client?

Exercise 10.1 Role play debriefing sheet

SOME ADDITIONAL COUNSELLING TECHNIQUES

Journals and diaries

Counselling is a therapy in which talking and the use of words allows for emotional expression and the appraisal and reappraisal of events, feelings, ideas and beliefs. A good deal of self-disclosure is implicit in this process and for some people this may be very threatening. Defence mechanisms, having been built up cannot and should not be disregarded; the client may need to use these as the only demonstration of being in charge of his/her life. This leaves the client with the problem of suppressed thoughts and feelings which may spill out in spite of the control mechanisms. For this person the diary or journal may provide a source of ventilation which does not require exposure to another human being.

For other people certain times of the day or night may become charged with emotion, when access to a listener is not possible. For them too, writing may be a way of externalising difficult thoughts and feelings.

The Gestalt method of addressing the 'empty chair' can also be achieved by people writing, as a letter, those things which they would like to have said, perhaps as a goodbye, or as the content of current pain, to the person who has died. The writing of a diary, journal, or letter may be an end in itself and for some people destroying the writing becomes a way of demonstrating their letting go. For others the documents become important records of the milestones in their grief and may be used to measure progress and to register particularly poignant periods in their grieving.

Pictures

We live in a world of visual images and these may evoke or express feelings and ideas which would be difficult to put into words This is especially true when working with children whose vocabulary and capacity for abstract thinking is not fully developed. Story books and pictures designed to use in exploring grief allow for events and feelings to be retold and reappraised.

Figure 11.1

Figure 11.1 was used in working with a six year old girl and prompted a very clear description of waiting outside the Intensive Care Unit following her brother's motor cycle accident. She was not allowed to see him and so for her the waiting consisted of wondering what he looked like, observing the distress of her mother, and being caught in the wider family drama which for her was experienced at a very mundane level, 'We were always looking in pockets and purses to find 10ps so that Mum could let the others know what was happening'. Her capacity to elaborate on experience was very limited without the picture prompts. For her not only could the 'story' be retold but the feelings acknowledged and appraised too; fears about the mutilating nature of her brother's injuries came to the surface, as did the anxieties about her mother's capacity to survive the trauma of his death.

SOME ADDITIONAL COUNSELLING TECHNIQUES

A child will also describe very effectively, through their own drawing, their perception of events and the impact of feelings upon them.

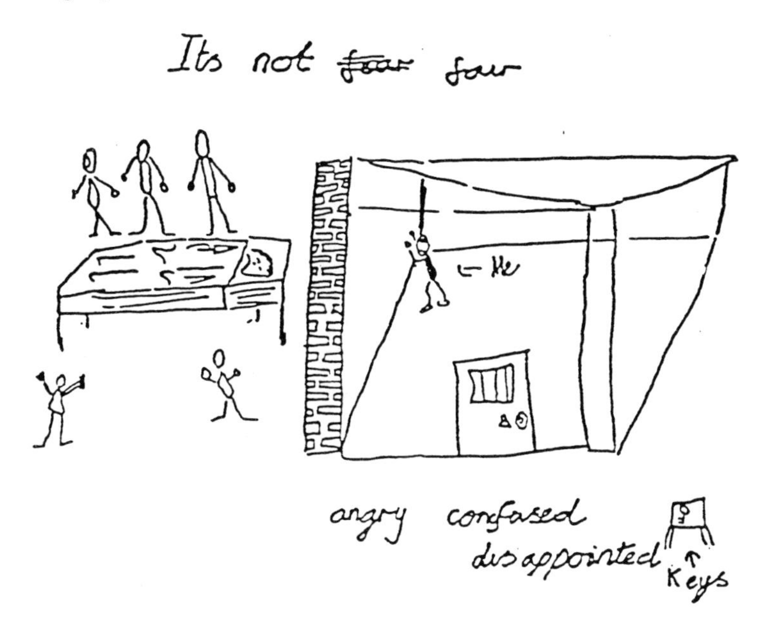

Figure 11.2

Words were hardly necessary to amplify the graphic illustration (Figure 11.2)made by a 10 year old boy about the anguish he felt when prevented from visiting his father on the hospital ward, just before his death. Equally his anger with God for 'picking my dad to die' (Figure 11.3).

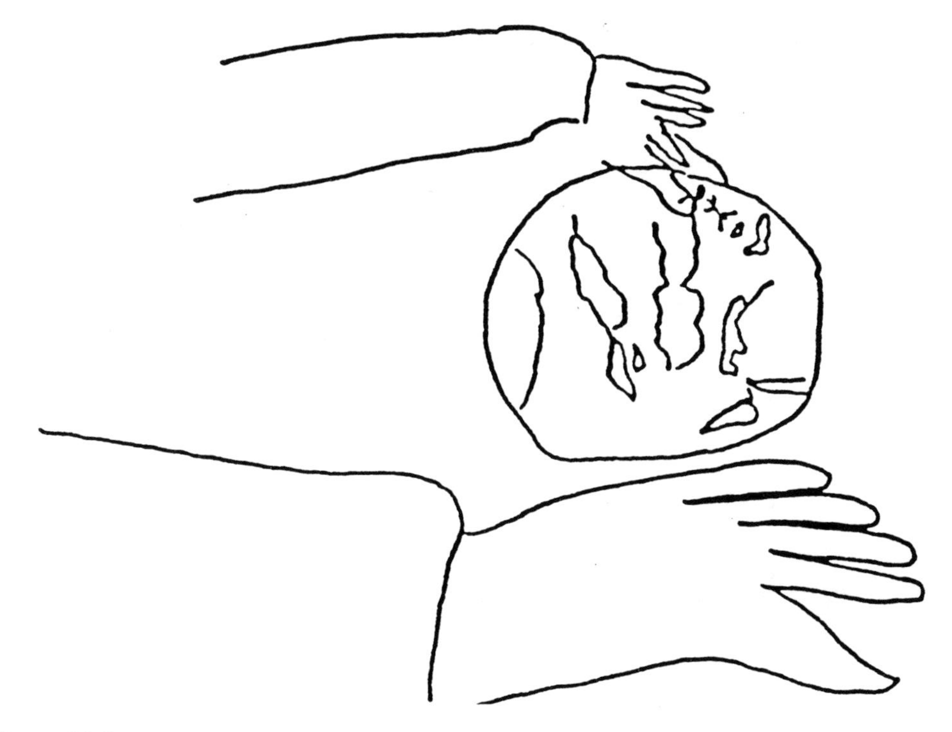

Figure 11.3

It is important when counselling a child or young person to use this as a means of communication, not as a method of psychological interpretation; it is simply a tool of dialogue between client and counsellor.

Sometimes it is fantasy not reality which needs to be explored, or the frightening territory of dreams which lies somewhere in between. The characteristics and powers of monsters and ghosts allow children to personify many fears which otherwise defy description.

SOME ADDITIONAL COUNSELLING TECHNIQUES

Figure 11.4

In Figure 11.4 a 10 year old could draw monsters but not describe his anxieties. Note the coffin shape at the centre which was the starting point in his picture. In addition to being a descriptive medium children will often visibly gain release from externalising thoughts and feelings in this way.

Photographs

We often underestimate the value of the family 'snap' until it becomes the only physical record of a person now dead. They are then prized as an important focal point for memory. Photographs are usually taken at happy events, family celebrations and holidays which can be the catalyst for the bittersweet recall of the happy memories but which remind us of 'what has been lost'. The pain of what is lost and yet the strength which comes from positive past relationships, produces a tension of opposite feelings for the bereaved.

For the counsellor this permits an important focus:

a) Upon that which has been lost
b) Upon the ego strengths that come from the relationship which the bereaved had with the deceased
c) Upon the pain which comes from handling this tension of opposite and frequently contradictory feelings.

Early in bereavement the client may find it difficult to remember what the loved person looked like. C. S. Lewis described this distressing state in *A Grief Observed*, in which he recognised that someone to whom one is close, may have been seen in so many situations that facial memory is difficult to capture. This problem may not be overcome even with photographs which in their static reality fail to conjure up the mobile, living face of the person now dead. People can be helped when they know that this is a common experience in bereavement and also given encouragement not to struggle with the problem of visual recall, because it does eventually return.

For some people photographs on display are a source of comfort while for others they may be too painful at certain stages in their grief. The counsellor can consider the place of photographs in the mourning process and directly use them as a medium of communication in their work with a client. At times photographs can be a useful tool for lightening or rounding off a counselling session.

Scrapbooks

Collecting together a variety of written and visual material connected with the person now dead can be a painful though therapeutic process of appraising the life and relationships of the deceased. It also leaves the bereaved with a record which is a precious document of their grief and a celebration of a loved person.

Family tree

Reappraising family dynamics and understanding the nature of past family interaction is an important part of recognising the impact of someone's death on the family group. What was the relationship of the deceased to individual members and what was his/her function within the total group? The smooth interaction of people within the family usually depends on certain of its members having communications and mediating roles within the group. Should one of these key figures die the others may be clear about their individual sense of loss but be confused by the overall disruption within the family. For example an elderly widower will be able to recognise the grief he feels for his wife but may feel confused about the distance which seems to have arisen between himself and his children, failing to see that it was his wife who previously was the agent of communications between himself and his children.

SOME ADDITIONAL COUNSELLING TECHNIQUES

As with many other aspects of grief, talking about this can help clarify what is happening. It is important that the counsellor is fully aware of these broader group dynamics in order to explore fully with the client ways in which the family has changed in its responses and interactions following someone's death. It can be very startling to discover that what had felt like a supportive caring group has become warring and disharmonious.

A useful technique in disclosing what is going on in the family is the drawing of a family tree or the use of counters or coins to show spatially what the comparative relationships are within the family. Using this method in which clients can have a spatial awareness of the relationship and connections of affection between people, can increase their appreciation of what is going on in the family now and what have been the past patterns within the family. This can be an important first step in perceiving what changes, modifications and new responses need to be made in the light of bereavement.

Bibliotherapy

Reference has already been made to the benefits which can come from writing journals and diaries as a way of externalising aspects of thinking and feeling, which have been painfully trapped within the mind and psyche of the bereaved peson. A similar liberating process can be achieved through reading literature, in story or poem form. Indeed one of the inherently cathartic experiences in an engagement with literaure, is the extent to which the reader identifies with the people and events within the 'story', and thus experiences emotions which are his/her own - not merely an objective encounter with a fictional world.

Bibliotherapy seeks to harness this relationship between literature and the emotional experience of the reader as a way of exploring and resolving feelings. It can be an important therapy in looking at such experiences as loss and separation – a feature of many life crises as well as bereavement. Dr Ofra Ayalon with colleagues in Israel has especially developed this as a technique for working with bereaved children, by gradually exposing them to different aspects of death and thus discovering their inner responses to it.

A variety of methods can be used to help identify and express the thoughts and feelings which have been elicited by the literature - role play, drawing or writing. It is a method which can be used in groups and with individuals, children and adults.

Relaxation

While bereavement counselling focuses upon painful events and feelings, and does not use the cultural avoidance technique of 'pulling yourself together', there are occasions when the client needs to rest from the heaviness of their emotions or establish an equilibrium which has been damaged in the face of persistent and confusing feelings. At this stage relaxation methods are a helpful way of affording a 'rest' or restoring 'equilibrium' and conveying a sense of order and control which can seem missing at certain distressing periods in bereavement.
There are a variety of sources including cassette tapes which suggest the procedure for relaxing and may be useful for the client to use as a routine for aiding relaxation and reducing stress.

BIBLIOTHERAPY

a) The leader/counsellor should assist the group/individual to be relaxed, ie find a comfortable, sitting position, body relaxed, eyes closed.
b) At this stage the story be read
c) Participants in the exercise are asked to imagine that they are one of the leaves in the story and to write a letter to the tree.
d) When this has been completed members put their letters into the centre of the group, pick out one written by someone else, and write a reply as if from the tree to the leaf. (Where the exercise is done with an individual, then he/she becomes respondent to their own initial letter).
e) When the response is finished group members should receive back their original letter with the reply. Time should be taken for people to read and assimilate the content of the replies.
f) Finally ask members to write an ending to the story.

The leaves were falling from the great oak at the meadow's edge. They were falling from all the trees.
One branch of the oak reached high above the others and stretched far out over the meadow. Two leaves clung to its very tip.
"It isn't the way it used to be", said one leaf to the other.
"No", the other leaf answered, "So many of us have fallen off tonight *we're almost the only ones left* on our branch".
"You never know who's going to go next" said the first leaf. "Even when it was warm and the sun shone, a storm or a cloudburst would come sometimes and many leaves were torn off, though they were still young. You never know who's going to go next."
"The sun seldom shines now," sighed the second leaf, "and when it does it gives no warmth. We must have warmth again."
"Can it be true", said the first leaf," can it really be true that *others come to take our places when we're gone* and after them still others, and more and more?"
"It is really true," whispered the second leaf. "We can't even begin to imagine it, it's beyond our powers."
"It makes me very sad," added the first leaf.
They were silent for a while. Then the first leaf said quietly to herself, *"Why must we fall? . . ."*
The second leaf asked, *"What happens to us* when we have fallen?"
"We sink down . . ."
'What is under us?"
The first leaf answered, "I don't know, some say one thing, some another, but nobody knows".
The second leaf asked, "Do we feel anything, do we know anything about ourselves when we're down there?"
The first leaf answered, "Who knows? *Not one of all those down there has ever come back to tell us about it.* "They were silent again. Then the first leaf said tenderly to the other, "Don't worry so much about it, you're trembling."
"That's nothing," the second leaf answered, "I tremble at the least thing now. I don't feel so sure of my hold as I used to."
"Let's not talk any more about such things," said the first leaf.
The other replied, "No, we'll let be. But - what else shall we talk about?" She was silent, but went on after a little while, "Which of us will go first?"
"There's still plenty of time to worry about that," the other leaf assured her. *"Let's remember how beautiful it was, how wonderful,* when the sun came out and shone so warmly that we thought we'd burst with life. Do you remember? And the morning dew, and the mild and splendid nights . . ."
"Now the nights are dreadful," the second leaf complained, "and there is no end to them."
"We shouldn't complain," said the first leaf gently. "We've outlived many, many others."
"Have I changed much?" asked the second leaf shyly but determinedly.
"Not in the least," the first leaf assured her. "You only think so because I've got to be so yellow and ugly. But it's different in your case."
"You're fooling me," the second leaf said.
"No, really," the first leaf exclaimed eagerly, "believe me, you're as lovely as the day you were born. Here and there may be a little yellow spot, but it's hardly noticeable and only makes you handsomer, believe me."
"Thanks," whispered the second leaf, quite touched. *"I don't believe you,* not altogether, but I thank you because you're so kind. You've always been so kind to me. I'm just beginning to understand how kind you are."
"Hush," said the other leaf, and kept silent herself for she was too troubled to talk any more.
Then they were both silent. Hours passed.
A moist wind blew, cold and hostile, through the tree-tops.
"Ah, now," said the second leaf, "I . . ." Then her voice broke off. She was torn from her place and spun down.

Winter had come.

Exercise 11.1 Bibliotherapy
Source Bambi by Felix Saltern (Jonathan Cape, London)
(The publishers gratefully acknowledge Jonathan Cape for their permission to use this extract)

RELAXATION

The client should be encouraged to adopt a comfortable position – sitting with their body fully supported in their chair, feet flat on the floor (preferably with shoes removed), and hands open and resting on their lap. The counsellor should use quiet, unhurried, calm speech to assist in creating a relaxed atmosphere.

Begin by asking the client to breathe deeply, letting out all the air in their lungs before taking another breath. Taking a deep sigh can be a helpful prelude to easier breathing if there is an inclination to inhale more air than is exhaled. Slowing down the pace of breathing – inhaling to a count of five and deeply exhaling to a count of five – begins to establish a rhythm which in itself is relaxing. Throughout the exercise keep returning to this focus on breathing, especially if the client has difficulty in naturally maintaining a smooth breathing pattern.

Continue the exercise by asking the client to lightly close their eyes and then work at relaxing all the muscles of the body. This is undertaken by consciously tensing the muscles as a prelude to relaxing them; by being aware of the contrasting sensation the client can begin to control the level of muscle tension and gradually assume a greater degree of relaxation. This process of tensing and relaxing the muscles should be done with the counsellor guiding the focus of the exercise until all parts of the body are relaxed - work from the head, face, shoulders, arms, chest, lower abdomen, buttocks, thighs, lower legs, feet. Work slowly and quietly through this process, gauging the individual client's capacity to achieve an effective state of relaxation.

When a relaxed state has been achieved it may help to retain a sense of calm by inviting the client to imagine themselves sitting in a warm, sunny, pleasant situation (they can mentally create the detail). Invite them to add pleasant sensory aspects to the picture in their mind - flowers, trees, birds, water lapping on a beach. Encourage them to 'stay' with the scene, gently experiencing the soothing sensations within the situation. Where this concentrated focus is difficult for a client suggest that they use a word, such as PEACE, to repeat slowly and as a replacement for other thinking which comes to mind unbidden during times of stress. Suggest a time eg five minutes, when you will cease guiding them through the relaxation and they can enjoy the peacefulness in an atmosphere of quiet.

At the end of the exercise ask the client to come back gradually to the present time – slowly opening their eyes and moving their body from the still position. It is important to allow time for this readjustment and a cup of tea can help in bringing the client to a re-engagement with the present.

This exercise can be beneficial to the client (and counsellor) at the end of an emotional session or during a particularly stressful period of life. They could be encouraged to go through the same process themselves, although it is always easier to be talked through the exercise.

Exercise 11.2 Relaxation

BEGINNINGS AND ENDINGS

Who am I as counsellor?

My starting point is me – my history, my potential; an amalgam of qualities which make me unique. Understanding the nature of that uniqueness requires that I am open to the same self-exploration as counselling demands of the client – a process which may be interesting at its least threatening, and profoundly painful at its most threatening. Experiencing the process of self-disclosure as well as learning from what is disclosed keeps me aware of the cost of being a client. As I become more practised as a counsellor it is easy to underestimate the courage needed by the client and I should attempt to keep my awareness alive by using supervision and/or peer group support as a way of remaining in touch with myself as 'client'. This empathy with the client role through being open to my own feelings and through awareness of my experience and the bearing this has on my perception and behaviour, allows for a sensitive engagement with my client when I am the counsellor.

Grief: the possibilities for growth

Each of us has developed strategies for dealing with loss (see Session 1). Whatever the individual blend of coping mechanisms it is important that these in no way obscure our understanding that:
a) Grief is natural and is a process of healing.
b) People possess the inner resources to survive and grow beyond their experience of loss.
c) A positive social context is a vital part of the external support needed by everyone who grieves.

These three principles must be the base from which we work as counsellors. If the counsellor's own experience, past or present, makes this difficult for him/her to accept then more time should be taken discovering the reasons for this. For anyone selecting counsellors it is important to appraise the would-be counsellor's responses to bereavement and styles of handling the experience. The Worden exercise (p 33) in *Grief Counselling and Grief Therapy* is a useful tool in exploring personal responses to grief and may highlight the painful issue of prospective grief as well as retrospective grief, which may not have been considered before. Consistent with the cultural tendency for avoidance this may be an area in which even the well-read student of grief and bereavement may find deep areas of unexplored feeling.

The cultural misunderstandings about grief, however challenged by the enlightenment of our knowledge about the way grief really operates, will be part of the inherited perception which counsellors bring to their work. This being so there may be times when we may seriously question how helpful it is for Mrs X to become 'so upset' in her session with us. It is important here for the counsellor to explore under supervision whether in fact Mrs X is appropriately expressing feelings that need to be ventilated or whether the chronic expression of her grief needs to be addressed by the challenge of 'letting go'. The latter is a totally different process from that of urging the mourner to 'pull themselves together', but rather is a process of helping the move, beyond the grief which has already exhaustively been expressed, into a new phase of adjustment. We must be sure in all these appraisals about the place unhelpful cultural wisdom plays in our thinking as against clear, rational insights.

Traditionally most caring roles carry very specific and well-identified tasks; the nurse engages in tasks which promote physical healing and comfort; the social worker seeks to improve the social conditions for his/her client often in a material way; the child minder makes practical provision for the safety, welfare and development of the children in her care. In all of these situations the need of those requiring care invites a specific response or intervention by the carer. We know that the act of caring is not wholly altruistic but it meets some of the carer's needs to be useful, needed, effective, liked, appreciated. In this sense counselling is different; it is most often passive, non-directional and provides no visible service. Within bereavement counselling it carries the added factor that we have no power to do what most clients wish, ie bring about the return of the deceased. Essentially we are working with the helplessness of the client and in many ways are confronted by our own helplessness. Those people who work as bereavement counsellors must be comfortable with this state of helplessness and not feel pulled into finding the more concrete gratification of other caring roles. The specifics of what we are doing in this situation stem from being available and not backing away from the emotional pain and social disruption of those who grieve. Frequent affirmation and support is necessary to sustain us in this role.

For the client the helplessness of losing a loved person through death can induce hopelessness, ie 'this is not merely a transitory phase of powerlessness but one from which I will never recover'. Profound loss and the devastating consequences of it can so shift the 'centredness' of life that the possibilities for restoring equilibrium, obscured by the grief itself, can seem quite impossible; the counsellor may in fact become infected with the client's sense of hopelessness. For the counsellor there needs to be a careful balance between hearing and accepting the blackness of 'now' while holding hope for the future, through belief in the healing nature of grief. That implicit sense of hopefulness must exist not as a grief-denying 'whistling in the dark', but as a truth about the nature of our ability to heal from grief; not a healing without scars but an ability to freshly take up life in the present.

Taking up life in the present involves letting go of the past. Throughout our lives we find ourselves facing situations where we need to say 'goodbye'. Sometimes they are short-lived or insignificant partings which make few emotional demands, but on other occasions we may be bidding a permanent farewell to a person or situation who/which has become important to our well being. Where this is so we may develop a number of avoidance techniques either to put off the parting or to act as if it had not taken place. This mirrors the denial which occurs in bereavement and may if persistent inhibit the process of coming to terms with loss. This process takes place when the bonds established within a group or the helping relationship with a client, come to and end and we need to:

BEGINNINGS AND ENDINGS

- confront the end
- appraise the 'journey', ie the process of shared experience
- acknowledge the loss

This can be painful, but like the pain of grief is a prelude to assimilating experience and moving on to a new phase of life. Helping a client successfully let go of the counselling relationship is the reward for a completed task and a demonstration of the importance of human autonomy as the end point of working through a major life crisis; interdependence is part of the human condition but periods of dependence which arise because of a particular need, rightfully should be time limited. Similarly human encounter of all kinds is transitory and subject to ending, therefore we need to practise letting go as a way of powerfully taking charge of the point of disengagement. A mature capacity to do this is characteristic of the person who is able to recognise and live confidently in the knowledge of their own resourcefulness and of their unique value as a human being.

Judy Tatelbaum in her book *The Courage to Grieve* says 'the goal of finishing is to move feelings or experiences from foreground to background, to gain relief, and to attain some shift in perspective'. This will happen where clients resolve grief, or where the counselling relationship comes to an end, or where the life of a group is concluded. Confronting the 'goodbye' will not only raise the pain of loss to the surface but will also bring the affirmation and mutual appraisal of a shared experience. The consequence of avoiding the pain is to miss the benefits of acknowledging the pleasure and triumphs of sharing 'the journey'.

Support

If self-awareness is an important preparation for counselling the bereaved, then support is a vital element in sustaining the on-going work with those who grieve. Receiving unburdened pain and listening to deep human tragedy calls on great reserves of sensitivity and humanity. Those reserves can only remain freshly available to each client if the counsellor has an opportunity to be supported in this stressful work. It is not an admission of weakness or failure but rather a means of retaining sharp sensitivity – not a response dulled by the need to defend oneself from the persisting onslaught of another's pain. Getting the support right will produce effective, sensitive counselling. As discussed in Session 8 supervision is essential for keeping clear the goals in counselling the client and defusing the confusion and stresses felt by the counsellor in working with the client. This is an important organisational task for counselling agencies and for the individual counsellor.

Conclusion

Working to be the best we can be as human beings, as well as counsellors, is our right and what our clients deserve from us.

BEGINNINGS AND ENDINGS

Respond to the following with reference to this group as a human forum for experience and not to comment on the course content.

1. How has learning with this group of people helped to meet the expectations you had at the beginning of the course?

2. How has working with this group of people made you feel good?

3. How has learning with this group of people been difficult?

4. What feelings are raised in you as you reflect on the group?

5. Are there any negative feelings, which need to be shared with the group? If yes, think clearly about what you would want to say to the group about them.

6. What positive feelings about the group as a whole do you want to share?

NB. These responses should be about the group as a whole not about individuals. Individual appreciations will be shared later.

They are confidential and should be seen as an opportunity to reflect honestly on the life of the group from your point of view. You can then select what to discuss in the full group.

Exercise 12.1 Responses to the course

BIBLIOGRAPHY

Session 1
Bowlby, John, 1981, *Loss*, Penguin
Marris, Peter, 1974, *Loss and Change*, RKP

Session 2
Jackson, Edgar, N., 1972, *The Many Faces of Grief*, SCM Press
Kubler-Ross, Elisabeth, 1973, *On Death and Dying*, Tavistock
Murray Parkes, Colin, 1972, *Bereavement*, Pelican

Session 3
Pincus, Lily, 1978, *Life and Death*, Abacus
Richardson, Jean, 1979, *A Death in the Family*, Lion

Session 4
Hollings, Michael, 1976, *Alive to Death*, Mayhew, McCrimmon
* Kushner, Harold S., 1982, *When Bad Things Happen to Good People*, Pan
* Purcell, William, 1978, *A Time to Die*, Mowbray
* Purcell, William, 1981, *Bereavement*, Mowbray
Speck, Peter, 1978, *Loss and Grief in Medicine*, Balliére Tindall
Speck, Peter, 1985, Religious and Cultural Aspects of Dying, *Bereavement Care*, Vol 4 No. 3 (Winter)
Tompkins, Susan (Ed), 1979, *Is Death the End?*, CEM

Session 5
Gentles, Ian (Ed), *Care of the Dying and the Bereaved*, Anglican Book Centre, Toronto
Gross Weizman, Savine and Kamm, Phyllis, 1987, *About Mourning*, Human Sciences Press Inc.
Raphael, Beverley, 1984, *The Anatomy of Bereavement*, Hutchinson
Raphael, Beverley, 1986, *When Disaster Strikes*, Hutchinson

Session 6
Blaiklock, E. M., 1980, *Kathleen*, Hodder and Stoughton
§ Craig, Mary, 1979, *Blessings*, Hodder and Stoughton
§ D'Arcy, Paula, 1979, *Song for Sarah*, Lion
Feehan, John M., 1972, *Tomorrow to be Brave*, Mercier Press
Frick, Marlena, 1972, *All the Days of His Dying*, Busbey, London
Humphrey, Derek, 1978, *Jean's Way*, Quartet
§ Leach, Christopher, 1981, *Letter to a Younger Son*, Dent
Lewis, C. S., 1961, *A Grief Observed*, Faber
Machin, Linda, 1980, *Living with Loss*, Lichfield Diocese
§ Schiff, Harriet Sarnoff, 1979, *The Bereaved Parent*, Condor
Vigeveno, H. S., 1977, *Dear David*, Regal, California
Zorza, Rosemary and Victor, 1980, *A Way to Die*, Andre Deutsch
Author anonymous, 1972, *Go Ask Alice*, Eyre Methuen

Session 7
Berger, William, 1974, *The Last Achievement*, Grail Pub
* DHSS, 1988, *What to do After a Death*, HMSO
Dyne, Geoffrey (Ed), 1981, *Bereavement Visiting*, King's Fund Pub
Matse, J. Nevejan, M. and Faber, H., 1971, *Bereavement*, Lutterworth
Smith, Carole, 1982, *Dying and Bereaved*, BASW
* Torrie, Margaret, 1970, *Begin Again*, Dent
Wright, Marion, 1987, *A Death in the Family*, Optima

Session 8
Biestek, Felix, 1961, *The Casework Relationship*, Allen and Unwin
Egan, Gerard, 1986, *The Skilled Helper*, Brooks/Cole Pub
Inskipp, Francesca, 1985, *A Manual for Trainers*, Alexia Pub
Kennedy, Eugene, 1977, *On Becoming a Counsellor*, Gill and MacMillan
Kennedy, Eugene, 1981, *Crisis Counselling*, Gill and MacMillan
Murgatroyd, Stephen, 1985, *Counselling and Helping*, Methuen
Noonan, Ellen, 1983, *Counselling Young People*, Methuen
Priestley, Philip and McGuire, James, 1983, *Learning to Help*, Tavistock

Session 9
Kennedy, Eugene, 1981, *Crisis Counselling*, Gill and MacMillan
Philpot, Terry (Ed), 1989, *Last Things*, Community Care
Worden, William, 1983, *Grief Counselling and Grief Therapy*, Tavistock

Session 10
Grollman, Earl, A. (Ed), 1967, *Explaining Death to Children*, Beacon Press, Boston
Foster, Suzanne and Smith, Pamela, 1987, *Brief Lives*, Arlington Books
Krementz, Jill, 1983, *How it Feels When a Parent Dies*, Victor Gollancz
Wells, Rosemary, 1988, *Helping Children Cope with Grief*, Sheldon Press
Worden, William, 1983, *Grief Counselling and Grief Therapy*, Tavistock

BIBLIOGRAPHY

Session 11

Ayalon, Ofra, 1987, *Rescue*, Nord Pub
Capacchione, Lucia, 1989, *The Creative Journal for Children*, Shambbala
Heegaard, Marge, 1988, *When Someone Very Special Dies*, Woodland Press, Minneapolis
Machin, Linda and Holt, Carole, 1988, *All Change*, CEM

Session 12

Tatelbaum, Judy, 1980, *The Courage to Grieve*, Cedar Books

Further reading

** Alix, Marlee and Benny, 1981, *Grandpa and Me*, Lion
Hill, Susan, 1977, *In the Springtime of the Year*, Penguin
** Burns, Peggy, 1987, *Far Side of the Shadow*, Harvestime
* McNeill Taylor, Liz, 1983, *Living with Loss*, Fontana
** Mellonie, Bryan and Ingpen, Robert, 1983, *Lifetimes*, Paper Tiger
** Selby, Jan 1975, *The Day Grandma Died*, CIO
** Smith, Doris, B., 1975, *A Taste of Blackberries*, Heinemann
* Snowden, Rita, 1977, *When Sorrow Comes*, Fountain
§ Stephens, Simon, 1972, *Death Comes Home*, Mowbrays
* Torrie, Margaret, 1976, *Caring for the Widow and Her Family*, CRUSE
** Viorst, Judith, 1974, *The Tenth Good Thing About Barney*, Collins
* Whitaker, Agnes (Ed), 1984, *All in the End is Harvest*, Darton, Longman and Todd
* Williams, Phillip , 1977, *Everlasting Spring*, Falcon
* Wood, Maurice, 1972, *Comfort in Sorrow*, Falcon
** Zoloton, C., 1974, *My Grandson Lew*, World's Work

* Books which the bereaved might find helpful
** Books for bereaved children
§ Books for bereaved parents

GENERAL NOTES

GENERAL NOTES